SCIENCE

Physical
Science

SADDLEBACK
EDUCATIONAL PUBLISHING

SCIENCE

Earth Science

Life Science

Physical Science

SADDLEBACK
EDUCATIONAL PUBLISHING
www.sdlback.com

ISBN-13: 978-1-62250-036-9
ISBN-10: 1-62250-036-9
eBook: 978-1-61247-679-7

Printed in the United States of America

17 16 15 14 13   9 10 11 12 13

Table of Contents

Drawing a Graph

A graph is often used to see if a relationship exists in a set of data. You can use a graph to show how one variable changes in response to another variable changing.

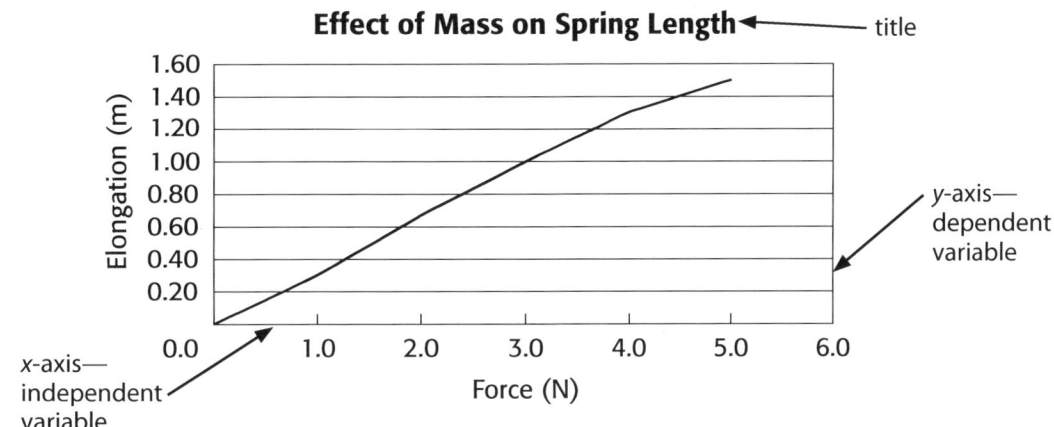

Data on the speed of an object during a certain time interval was collected and placed in a data table. Follow the steps below to graph the data.

Step 1   Draw an *x*-axis and a *y*-axis.

Step 2   Label the *x*-axis with the independent variable—this is the variable you change.

Step 3   Label the *y*-axis with the variable that is the dependent variable—the variable that is a result of changing a variable.

Step 4   Decide on the scale for each axis. Look at your data. Determine the range of the data for each axis. Choose a scale that has the numbers equally spaced.

Step 5   Plot each point.

Step 6   Draw a line connecting the data points.

Time (s)	Speed (m/s)
0	0
10	20
20	45
30	60
40	84

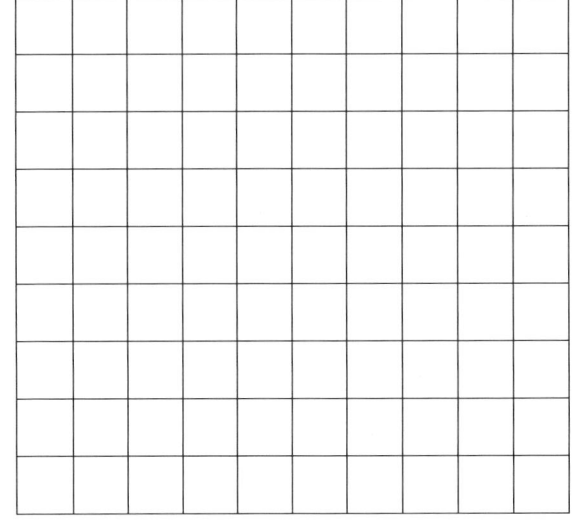

Reading a Graph

Data collected in an experiment is often displayed on a graph. A graphical display can be an easy way to see the relationship between variables.

1. When both variables increase the trend is _____.

2. When one variable increases and the other decreases the trend is _____.

3. When there is no relationship between variables there is _____

   between variables.

Use the graph to answer the following questions.

4. What are the two variables tested in this experiment? _____

5. The horizontal axis (the axis that goes from left to right) is known as the *x*-axis.

   The independent variable is placed along the *x*-axis. What is the independent variable?

   _____

6. The vertical axis (the axis that goes up and down) is the *y*-axis. The dependent variable is placed along the *y*-axis. What is the dependent variable?

   _____

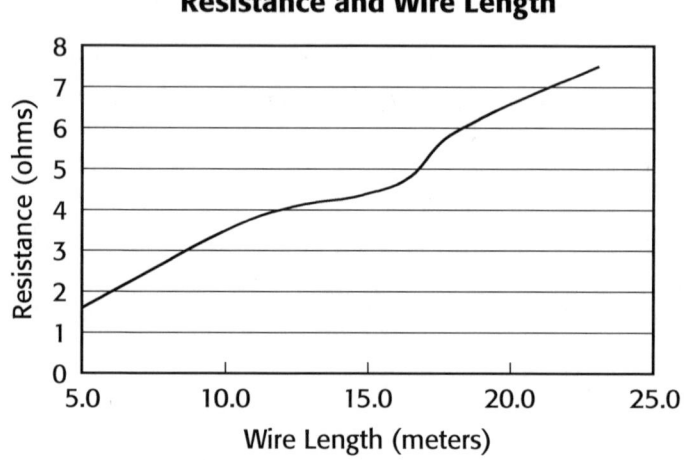

Resistance and Wire Length

7. To read a point on the graph, start at the *x*-axis, move up the line, move across to the *y*-axis, and read the point on the *y*-axis. What is the resistance in a 15 m piece of wire? _____

8. What do you notice about the graph as the length of the wire increases?

   _____

9. Is this a positive or negative trend? _____

10. Based on the graph, what will happen if the length of the wire is increased to 25 m?

   _____

Organizing Data

Before you actually conduct your experiment, you need to decide how you will record what happens during the experiment. Often you record data in a science notebook. After you have gathered your data, you need to decide on a way to organize the data to present to others that want to see what you have gathered. Your data must be organized in an orderly way. You can follow the steps below to organize the data from the following experiment.

0 minutes: sand = 20.5°C; water = 20.5°C
1 minute: sand = 20.9°C; water = 20.7°C
2 minutes: water = 20.9°C; sand = 21.5°C
3 minutes: water = 21.2°C; sand = 22.0°C
4 minutes: sand = 22.6°C; water = 21.4°C
5 minutes: water = 21.6°C; sand = 23.2°C

Creating a data table will be the easiest way to organize your data. When you create a data table to organize your data, the independent variable is at the heading of the first column.

Step 1 Place the name of the independent variable in the top of the left column.

Step 2 Place the headings of the dependent variable at the top of the middle and right columns.

Step 3 Enter the data for each dependent variable in its correct column. In other words, place all the sand data in the sand column and the water data in the water column.

1.	2.	3.
4.	20.5°C	20.5°C
5.	20.7°C	20.9°C
6.	20.9°C	21.5°C
7.	21.2°C	22.0°C
8.	21.4°C	22.6°C
9.	21.6°C	23.2°C

(Identifying Variables in an Experiment

In an experiment, you make changes in a situation and see the results. The conditions set in an experiment are known as the *variables*. A variable can be temperature, the amount of water, or amount of food given each day. In an experiment, only one factor (variable) should change. This variable is known as the *independent variable*. The result of your experiment is the *dependent variable*.

The following sample experiment tests the effect of slope of a ramp on how fast a marble goes.

- Make a ramp with a single piece of wood.
- Raise the ramp to a height of 10 cm.
- Place a piece of tape 40 cm from the bottom of the ramp.
- Place a marble at the top of the ramp.
- Release the marble and record the time it takes the marble to reach the piece of tape.
- Raise the ramp 5 cm and determine the time it takes the marble to reach the tape. Repeat for additional heights of the ramp.

1. List all the possible factors, or variables, in the experiment. _____

_____

_____

2. Which of these variables stayed the same in each trial? _____

_____

_____

3. Which variable was different in each trial? _____

4. Is this the independent or dependent variable? _____

5. You observe that it takes less time for the marble to reach the tape as the height of the

ramp increases. Is the time it takes the marble to reach the tape the independent or

dependent variable? _____

6. List your variables in an experiment in which you explore if the mass of the

marble affects the time it takes to reach the tape. Which variables would change?

_____

_____

_____

Designing an Experiment

When a scientist asks a question, the search for the answer to that question leads to a hypothesis. To test that hypothesis, a scientist will design an experiment. When designing an experiment you need to consider the following:

- the variable being tested,
- the variable being recorded,
- other variables that need to be the same all the time during the experiment.

A scientist wants to determine if the time it takes a certain amount of salt to dissolve changes with a change in temperature. The experiment is set up with two test tubes half full of 25°C water.

Answer the following questions regarding the variables in this experiment.

1. What are the variables being tested? _____
_____

2. Which variable is easier to change? This will be the independent variable. _____
_____

3. Which variable will be the dependent variable? _____

4. List the other variables you need to consider. The list is started for you—name four

additional variables.

- Size of the test tube
- Amount of water
- _____

- _____
- _____
- _____

Place the steps of the experiment in order. Write *1* in the blank next to the step that comes first, *2* in the space next to the step that comes second, and so on.

5. _____ Add 10 g of salt to the water in each test tube. Do not shake the tubes.

6. _____ As you add the salt, start a timer. Record the time it takes all of the salt to dissolve in the water.

7. _____ Empty the test tubes. Completely clean and dry the tubes. Add 25 mL of water 15°C to each tube. Add 10 g of salt and record the time it takes the salt to dissolve.

8. _____ Label five identical test tubes 1–5. Place them in a test tube rack.

9. _____ Place 25 mL of water at 25°C into each test tube.

Drawing Conclusions

Once you have recorded the results of an experiment, you must review the data to see if any patterns or relationships exist. From the patterns that exist, you can draw a conclusion, or make a statement about the relationships that exist between your variables.

The data in the tables below show the number of swings of a pendulum in 15 seconds. In the first table, the length changed (with a constant mass). In the second table, the mass changed (but the length of the pendulum remained the same).

Draw a conclusion regarding the data in the tables. Answer the questions by filling in the blanks.

Pendulum Length (cm)	Swings
5	32
10	23
20	17
40	12
60	9

1. What happens to the number of swings of the pendulum when the length increases from 5 cm to 10 cm? _____

   _____

2. What happens to the number of swings of the pendulum when the length increases from 10 cm to 15 cm? _____

   _____

3. Does this trend continue for the remaining pendulum lengths? _____

4. What happens to the number of swings of the pendulum when the mass increases from 5 g to 10 g?

   _____

   _____

Pendulum Mass (g)	Swings
5	23
10	23
20	22
40	24
60	23

5. Does this trend continue for the remaining pendulum masses? _____

6. What can you say about the number of swings of the pendulum and the length and mass of the pendulum? _____

   _____

   _____

(*Predicting*

When you make a logical deduction based on evidence presented, you are predicting. When you predict, you look at a set of data and based upon trends shown in the data, conclude what will happen in a future event.

When you predict, you follow these steps:

Step 1 Gather information or data.

Step 2 Consider possible outcomes.

Step 3 Consider the evidence to find the most likely outcome.

In an experiment the same force is applied to blocks of ice with different masses. The acceleration of each block is measured. The table below shows the results of the experiment.

Mass (kg)	Acceleration (m/s²)
1.0	3.0
1.5	2.0
2.0	1.5
2.5	1.2
3.0	1.0
3.5	0.86
4.0	0.75

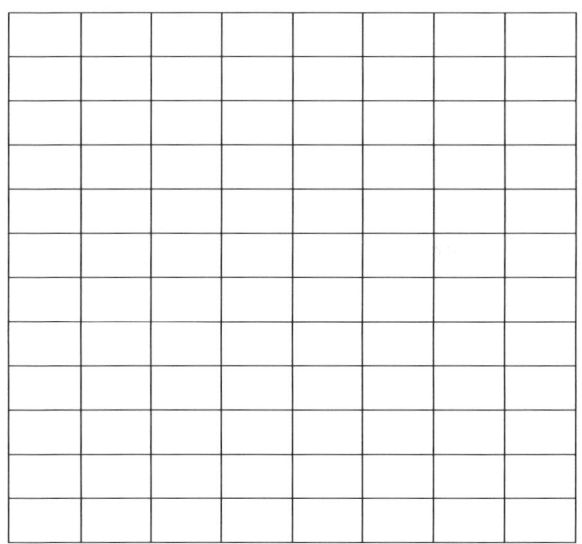

Use the data above to draw a graph and answer the following questions.

1. What are you comparing? _____

_____

2. How does the acceleration change as the mass changes? _____

_____

3. When one quantity changes in one direction, and the other changes in the opposite direction, this is a negative relationship. Is this a negative relationship?

_____

4. Based on the trend given on the graph, extend the line graph to 6.0 kg. What is the acceleration for 6.0 kg? _____

Analyzing Data

When you analyze data you follow these steps:

Step 1 Identify your variables.

Step 2 Look at the sets of data—what happens when going from one set to the next.

Step 3 Determine if a relationship exists between the variables.

Step 4 Determine if the relationship holds true in all situations.

The table below shows the number of tacks picked up by two magnets. Analyze the data by answering the following questions.

1. What are the variables tested in this experiment? _____

   _____

   _____

2. Name the independent variable(s).

   _____

   _____

3. Name the dependent variable(s).

   _____

   _____

Battery Voltage (V)	Number of Tacks	
	10-Turn Magnet	20-Turn Magnet
0	0	0
1.5	3	7
3.0	6	13
4.5	8	17
6.0	12	23

4. How many tacks are picked up at 1.5 V? _____

5. What happens to the number of tacks picked up when the voltage increases to 3.0 V?

   _____

6. Does this trend continue for both types of magnets when the voltage increases

   to 4.5 V? _____

7. How many tacks are picked up by the 10-turn magnet at 1.5 V? _____

   How many tacks are picked up by the 20-turn magnet at the same voltage? _____

8. Examine the number of tacks picked up by each magnet at the various voltages.

   What can you conclude about the number of tacks picked up versus the number

   of turns? _____

   _____

Physical Science • © Saddleback Educational Publishing • www.sdlback.com

Converting SI Units

Measurement in SI is based on powers of 10. Each unit is 10 times larger or 10 times smaller than the next unit. The table below shows the different SI prefixes and their meaning. Because SI measurement is based on powers of 10, converting from one unit to another is easy if you remember the rules below.

Multiply by	Move the decimal point	Divide by	Move the decimal point
1,000	3 places to the right	1,000	3 places to the left
100	2 places to the right	100	2 places to the left
10	1 place to the right	10	1 place to the left
0.1	1 place to the left	0.1	1 place to the right
0.01	2 places to the left	0.01	2 places to the right
0.001	3 places to the left	0.001	3 places to the right

When you multiply from a smaller unit to a larger unit you divide by the multiple of 10 separating the units. To convert from a larger unit to a smaller unit you multiply by the multiple of 10 separating the units.

How many millimeters are there in 250 centimeters?

Step 1 What is your starting unit?   Start: centimeters

Step 2 What is your ending unit?   End: millimeters

Step 3 What is the multiple of 10 separating   Millimeters and centimeters are next to each
the units?   other, so they are separated by a factor of 10.

Step 4 Are you going from a larger unit to   Large (centimeters) to small (millimeters)
a smaller unit, or smaller to larger?

Step 5 Do you multiply or divide your   Multiply
multiple of 10?

Step 6 Solve by moving the decimal point.   Move the decimal point 1 place to the right.
                                                          250.0 = 2500. or 2,500 millimeters

Convert the following:

1. 100 cm to m _____   **2.** 25 mg to cg _____

3. 10 mg to cg _____   **4.** 100 mm to km _____

5. 1.5 km to m _____   **6.** 1,475 mg to g _____

Scientific Method

Trace the steps of the scientific method by completing the flow chart.

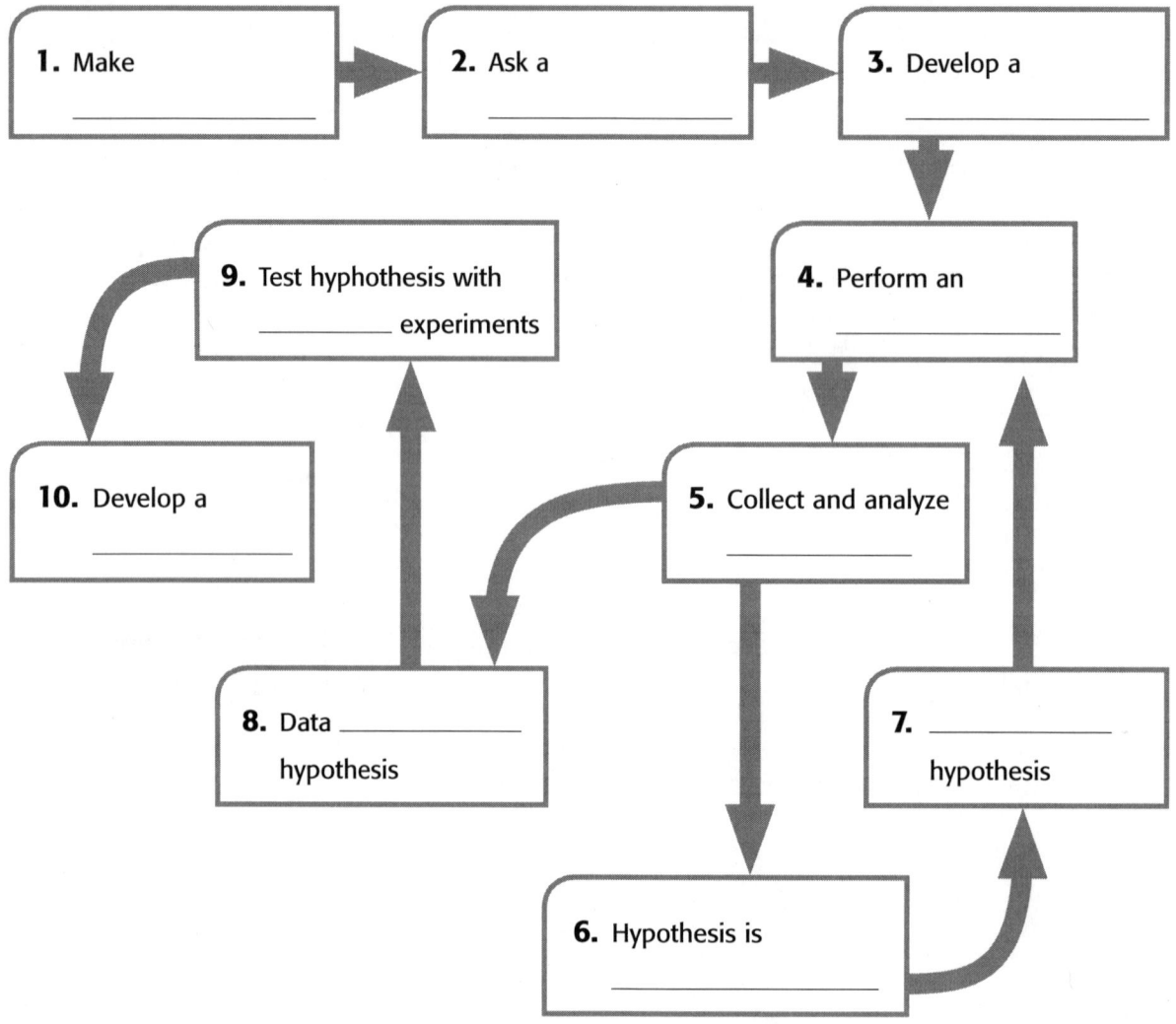

Identify the steps in solving the following scientific problem:
Find out which brand of light bulb lasts the longest.

11. _____   You use three identical lamps, plugged into three identical sockets.

12. _____   You turn on the lights at the same time and time how long each lamp stays lit.

13. _____   You are curious as to whether all brands of light bulbs last the same amount of time.

14. _____   The data indicates that not all brands of bulbs are the same, some last longer than others.

15. _____   You record the number of hours each bulb lasts.

Elements, Compounds, and Mixtures

All matter is classified into one of three categories. Explore the classification of matter by completing the concept map below.

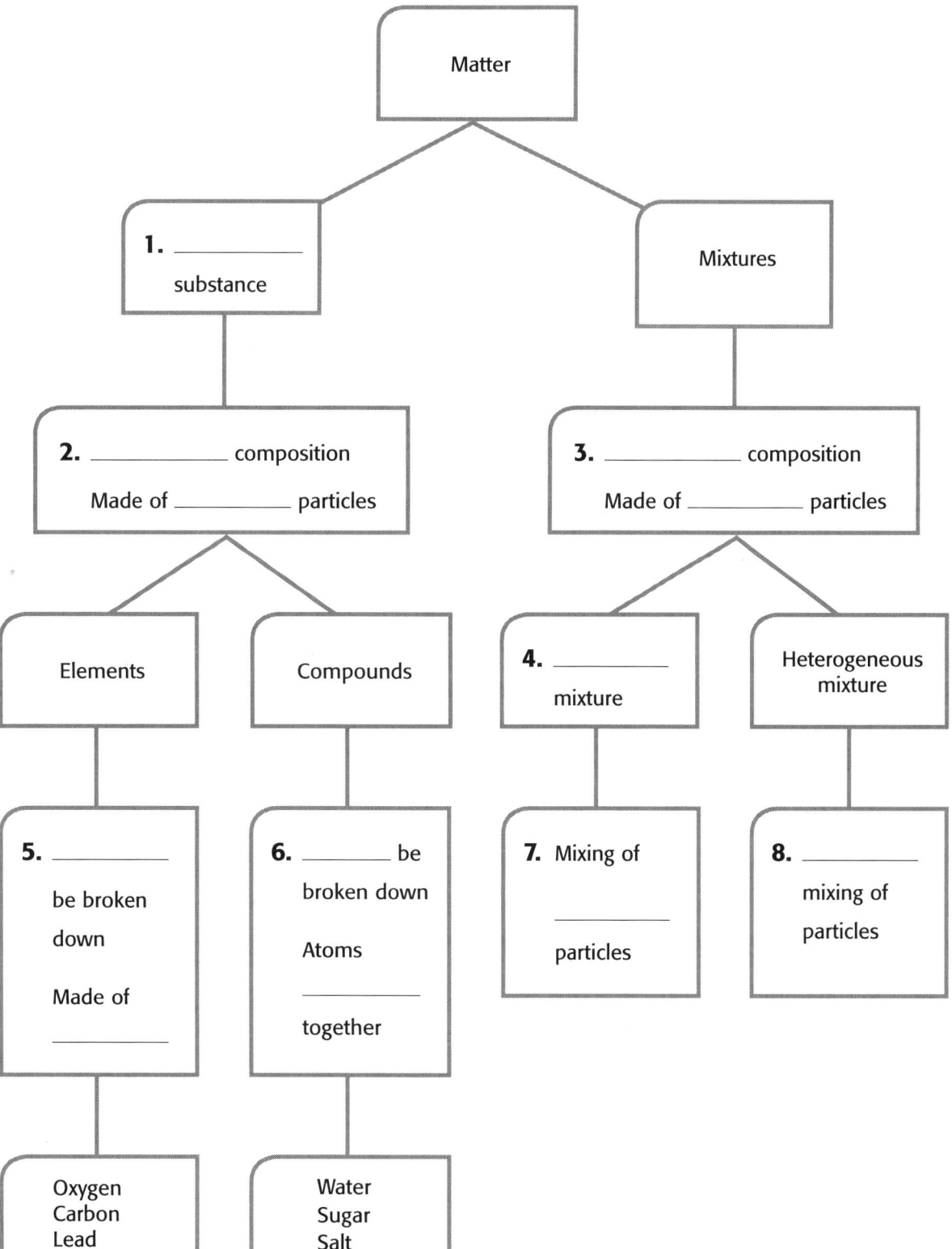

Matter

1. _____
   substance

Mixtures

2. _____ composition
   Made of _____ particles

3. _____ composition
   Made of _____ particles

Elements

Compounds

4. _____
   mixture

Heterogeneous mixture

5. _____
   be broken down
   Made of
   _____

6. _____ be broken down
   Atoms
   _____
   together

7. Mixing of
   _____
   particles

8. _____
   mixing of particles

Oxygen
Carbon
Lead

Water
Sugar
Salt

Physical and Chemical Properties

When you make observations about the properties of a material you are observing one of two types of properties. One type of property of a material is a physical property. A *physical property* is a feature you can observe or measure without changing the identity of the material. A *chemical property* is a feature that describes the material's interaction with another substance, often resulting in a change that produces a new substance.

Classify each property as a chemical or a physical property. Write C in the blank if the property is a chemical property and P if the property is a physical property.

1. _____ Reacts with oxygen.

2. _____ A metal tarnishes in the presence of alcohol.

3. _____ Water is a liquid at room temperature.

4. _____ An iron gate rusts in the presence of oxygen and water.

5. _____ The boiling point of water is 212°F.

6. _____ The density of water is 1 g/cm^3.

7. _____ An acid is a substance that tastes sour.

8. _____ Gold is a metal; metals are shiny.

9. _____ Hydrochloric acid reacts with a metal to produce hydrogen.

10. _____ Ten milliliters of water has a mass of 10 grams.

11. _____ Gasoline vapors are flammable, reacting with oxygen and producing heat.

12. _____ Gold is a metal that does not react with oxygen.

Read the following description of the element sodium. Then list all the chemical and physical properties mentioned in the reading.

13. Mercury(II) oxide is a bright red or orange red compound. It is odorless. It is a crystalline solid at room temperature. This compound when exposed to light or is heated to 500°C decomposes to form mercury and oxygen gas. It dissolves in diluted nitric acid or hydrochloric acid, but it is insoluble in water.

_____

_____

_____

_____

Physical Science • © Saddleback Educational Publishing • www.sdlback.com

Physical and Chemical Changes

Matter can undergo many changes. These changes are either chemical in nature or physical. A *chemical change* is a change in which a new substance is formed. A *physical change*, on the other hand results in a change in appearance, but does not result in the formation of a new substance.

You can recognize a chemical change or physical change by one or more clues. Each situation describes a chemical or physical change. For each, complete the statement that cites the evidence of change.

Physical Change	Evidence of a Change
Ice melts.	**1.** A change in _____ is evidence of a physical change.
Sugar is placed in water and disappears.	**2.** A solid _____ into a liquid is evidence of a physical change.
In an ice pack one substance dissolves into another, the pack gets cold.	**3.** A change in _____ is evidence of a physical change.
An artist hammers a piece of copper into a thin sheet.	**4.** A change in _____ is evidence of a physical change.
A sugar cube is crushed into smaller pieces.	**5.** A piece of matter broken into _____ pieces is evidence of a physical change.

Chemical Change	Evidence of a Change
Vinegar is dropped on baking soda; there is fizzing and the production of carbon dioxide, a gas.	**6.** Formation of a _____ is evidence of chemical change.
Gray-colored iron rusts in the presence of oxygen and water.	**7.** A change in _____ is evidence of a chemical change.
Two clear liquids are mixed together, producing a solid that settles on the bottom of the container.	**8.** The production of a _____ is evidence of a chemical change.
Natural gas burns on a stove to heat water.	**9.** The release or absorption of _____ is evidence of a chemical change.

◖ Density

You have been given several different sized samples of the mineral quartz. You measure the mass and the volume of each sample. The data is recorded in the table below.

For each sample, divide the mass by the volume. Record the result of each calculation in the right column.

Sample	Mass	Volume	Mass/Volume
1	10 g	3.85 cm^3	**1.**
2	15 g	5.76 cm^3	**2.**
3	20 g	7.70 cm^3	**3.**
4	25 g	9.61 cm^3	**4.**
5	30 g	11.5 cm^3	**5.**
6	35 g	13.5 cm^3	**6.**
7	40 g	15.4 cm^3	**7.**

8. What do you notice about the value of each result? _____

_____

9. The mass divided by the volume equals a quantity known as *density*. Another way

of looking at density is that it is the amount of matter (mass) in a given amount of

space (volume). For quartz, does the mass divided by the volume always equal

2.6 g/cm^3? _____

10. To calculate the density you can use this formula: D = m/v. If you have a 5 g sample

of magnetite, the sample has a volume of 0.9 cm^3. What is the density of magnetite?

_____

11. Suppose you cut the magnetite sample in half. What is the density of each piece?

_____

12. You have a sample of fluorite that has a volume of 15 cm^3. Fluorite has a density of

3.2 g/cm^3. What is the mass of the sample? _____

Physical Science • © Saddleback Educational Publishing • www.sdlback.com

Solids, Liquids, and Gases

Compare the different states of matter by completing the table below.

	Solid	Liquid	Gas
Shape	1.	2.	3.
Volume	4.	5.	6.
Compressibility	7.	8.	9.
Expansion or Heating	10.	11.	12.

Classify each statement as true or false. If the statement is true, place a *T* in the blank. If the statement is false, place an *F* in the blank and replace the underlined term with one that will make the statement true.

13. _____ Particles in a solid are spread far apart. _____

14. _____ The resistance of a liquid to flowing is known as viscosity. _____

15. _____ A liquid will take the shape of the container in which it is placed. _____

16. _____ The temperature at which a solid changes to a liquid is the solid's boiling point. _____

17. _____ The temperature of a gas is the force exerted by the gas particles on the wall of its container. _____

18. _____ The particles of a solid stay in fixed positions, resulting in the solid having a definite shape and volume. _____

19. _____ The particles in a liquid move freely around and past each other. _____

20. _____ In an amorphous solid the particles of the solid are arranged in a regular pattern. _____

21. _____ The particles of a liquid will spread out to fill all the space in the container into which it is placed. _____

22. _____ When a liquid moves from one container to another it's volume does not change. _____

Boyle's Law

Data was collected during an experiment that investigated the relationship between the volume of a gas and the pressure exerted by the gas. During the experiment the amount and the temperature of the gas did not change.

Reading	Pressure (kPa)	Volume (L)
1	150	0.334
2	200	0.250
3	250	0.200
4	300	0.167
5	350	0.143

The relationship between the volume and pressure of a gas is known as *Boyle's Law*. Use the data above to state Boyle's Law.

1. When the pressure of a gas is _____ at a constant temperature, the

   volume of the gas decreases. When the pressure of the gas _____

   at a constant temperature, the volumes increases.

A gas occupies a volume of 50 mL and exerts a pressure of 101 kPa. The volume of the gas increases to 75 mL under a constant temperature. What is the new pressure of the gas?

Step 1 What do you know?   First volume (V_1): 50 mL

                                                               First pressure (T_1): 101 kPa

                                                               Second volume (V_2): **2.** _____

Step 2 What are you trying to find?   The second pressure (P_2)

Step 3 What formula can you use? $P_1V_1 = P_2V_2$

Step 4 Use the numbers in the formula and solve.   (50 mL)(101 kPa) = **3.** _____

Step 5 Divide both sides in the equation by $P_2 = 67.33$ kPa

   4. _____ .

5. A gas occupies a volume of 40 ml and exerts a pressure of 101 kPa. The pressure

   is increased to 150 kPa under a constant temperature. What is the new volume of

   the gas? _____

Physical Science • © Saddleback Educational Publishing • www.sdlback.com

Charles's Law

Data was collected during an experiment that investigated the relationship between the volume of a gas and its temperature. During the experiment the amount of gas and the pressure of the gas did not change.

Reading	Volume (mL)	Temperature (K)
1	750	375
2	700	350
3	650	325
4	600	300
5	550	275

The relationship between the volume and temperature of a gas is known as *Charles's Law.* **Use the data above to state Charles's Law.**

1. When the temperature of a gas is _____ at a constant pressure, the

volume of the gas increases. When the temperature of the gas _____

at a constant pressure, the volume decreases.

A gas at 25°C occupies a volume of 50 mL. The temperature increases to 40°C. Assuming the pressure does not change, what is the new volume of the gas?

Step 1 What do you know?

(You must change from 0°C to K by adding 273 to the temperature in °C.)

First temperature (T_1): 25°C = 298 K

First volume (V_1): **2.** _____

Second temperature (T_2): 40°C = 313 K

Step 2 What are you trying to find?

The second volume (V_2)

Step 3 What formula can you use?

3. _____

Step 4 Use the numbers in the formula and solve.

$$\frac{50 \text{ mL}}{298 \text{ K}} = \frac{V_2}{313 \text{ K}}$$

Step 5 Multiply both sides of the equation by 313.

$P_2 = 52.52$ mL

4. A gas at 50°C has a volume of 100 mL. The volume of the gas increases to 150 mL under

constant pressure. What is the new temperature of the gas? _____

◖ The Combined Gas Law

The relationships between pressure, volume, and temperature can be expressed by a single equation. This equation combines Boyle's Law and Charles's Law and is known as the Combined Gas Law. The Combined Gas Law is:

$$\frac{P_1 V_1}{T_1} = \frac{P_2 V_2}{T_2}$$

A container is holding a gas at 300 kPa, 0.25 L, and 0°C. Later, the same gas undergoes a change in pressure to 100 kPa and temperature to 25°C. What is the new volume of the gas?

Step 1 What do you know?

(Remember to change from 0°C to K by adding 273 to the temperature in °C.)

First pressure (P_1): 300 kPa

First volume (V_1): 0.25 L

First temperature (T_1): 0°C = 273 K

Second pressure (P_2): 100 kPa

Second temperature (T_2): 25°C = 298 K

Step 2 What are you trying to find?

The second volume (V_2)

Step 3 What formula can you use?

$$\frac{P_1 V_1}{T_1} = \frac{P_2 V_2}{T_2}$$

Step 4 Use the numbers in the formula and solve.

$$\frac{(300 \text{ kPa})(0.25 \text{ L})}{273 \text{K}} = \frac{(100 \text{ kPa}) V_2}{298 \text{ K}}$$

$$V_2 = 0.819 \text{ L}$$

1. A gas at 125 kPa and 30°C has a volume of 2.0 L. The temperature is raised to 50°C and the pressure is increased to 400 kPa. What is the new volume? _____

2. A gas at 0°C and 100 kPa has a volume of 2.5 L. The temperature of the gas is lowered to −25°C and the volume is decreased to 1.0 L. What is the new pressure of the gas?

_____

3. A gas at an unknown temperature occupies 1.5 L and has a pressure of 50 kPa. The volume of the gas is lowered to 0.75 L and the pressure increases to 125 kPa at 50°C. What was the original temperature of the gas? _____

Physical Science • © Saddleback Educational Publishing • www.sdlback.com

Changes of State

Trace the different changes of state by completing the flow chart below.

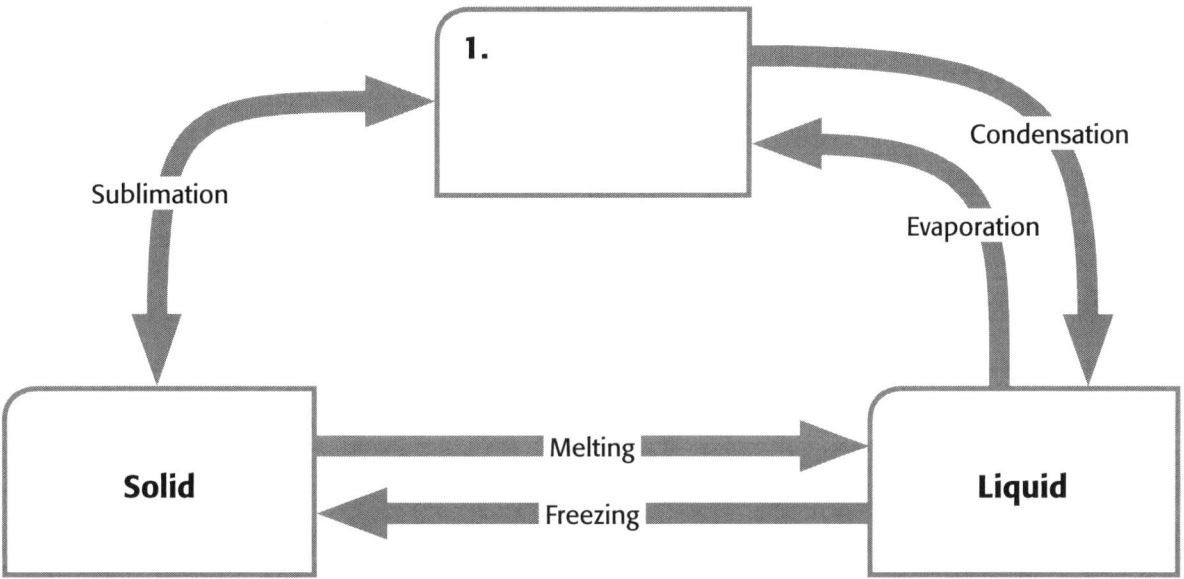

For each statement, place a _T_ in the space if the statement is true. Place an _F_ in the space if the statement is false. For each false statement, replace the underlined term with a term that will make the statement true.

2. _____ The change of state from solid to a liquid is <u>freezing</u>. _____

3. _____ When thermal energy is added to a substance at its boiling point, the temperature of that substance will <u>increase</u>. _____

4. _____ Thermal energy added to a substance goes towards <u>increasing</u> the motion of the particles of the substance. _____

5. _____ When a liquid changes to a gas at the substance's boiling point, thermal energy added to the particles help them move <u>together</u> and become a gas. _____

6. _____ The melting point (temperature) of a substance and the freezing point (temperature) of a substance <u>is the same</u> temperature. _____

7. _____ Evaporation and boiling are terms that describe a liquid changing state to a <u>solid</u>. _____

8. _____ The boiling point (temperature) of a liquid changes with air pressure. When the air pressure decreases, the boiling point <u>decreases</u>. _____

9. _____ The opposite of evaporation is <u>condensation</u>. _____

☾ Heating Curves

Explore what happens to a substance that starts as a solid and has thermal energy added to the substance over time.

Heating Curve for Water

Use the graph above to complete each statement below. For each statement, circle the term in the pair that makes the statement true.

1. At location A the substance is a [solid / gas].

2. At point A the temperature of the substance is [decreasing / increasing].

3. At point B the addition of thermal energy [continues / stops].

4. At point B the temperature of the substance is [increasing / steady].

5. At point B the substance is changing state, going from a solid to a liquid. During a change of state, the temperature [stays the same / increases]. The temperature at which the change of state occurs is the [boiling / melting] point.

6. At location C the substance is a [solid / liquid].

7. At point C the temperature of the substance is [decreasing / increasing].

8. At point D the addition of thermal energy [continues / stops] the process.

9. At point D the temperature of the substance is [increasing / steady].

10. At point D the substance is changing state, going from a liquid to a gas. During a change of state, the temperature [stays the same / increases].

11. The temperature at which the change of state occurs is the [boiling / melting] point.

Physical Science • © Saddleback Educational Publishing • www.sdlback.com

Structure of the Atom

Compare the different parts of the atom by completing the table below.

	Proton	Neutron	Electron
Discovered 1st, 2nd, 3rd	1.	2.	3.
Mass (in atom mass units—amu)	4. _____ amu	5. _____ amu	6. 0 _____
Charge	7. __1	0	8. __1
Location in the atom	9.	10.	11.
Symbol	12.	13.	14.

The current model of the atom says that electrons are found in regions surrounding the nucleus. These regions, called *energy levels,* hold a certain number of electrons.

Complete the table below by distributing electrons to the new ion energy levels. Remember to fill the levels in order starting with the lowest.

Elements	Number of Electrons	Electrons in 1st Energy Level	Electrons in 2nd Energy Level	Electrons in 3rd Energy Level	Electrons in 4th Energy Level
Lithium	3	2	1	N/A	N/A
Flourine	9	15.	16.	N/A	N/A
Beryllium	4	17.	18.	N/A	N/A
Calcium	20	19.	20.	21.	22.
Sodium	11	23.	24.	25.	N/A
Phosphorus	15	26.	27.	28.	N/A
Oxygen	8	29.	30.	N/A	N/A

Models of the Atom

Explore the different models of the atom by completing the tables below.

Dalton's Model	
Proposed:	Early 1800s
Particles included:	**1.**
Description:	**2.** All matter is made of tiny particles called _____.
Why did it not work?	**3.** Did not account for _____ and _____.

Thomson's Model	
Proposed:	Late 1800s
Particles included:	**4.**
Description:	**5.** The atom is a _____ charged sphere with _____ embedded in the sphere.
Why did it not work?	**6.** Did not account for the _____.

Rutherford's Model	
Proposed:	Early 1900s
Particles included:	**7.** _____ and _____
Description:	**8.** Protons are found together in a _____; the _____ surround the nucleus.
Why did it not work?	Did not explain how the electrons orbited the nucleus.

Bohr's Model	
Proposed:	Early 1900s
Particles included:	**9.** _____ and _____
Description:	**10.** Protons are found together in a _____; the electrons move in _____ around the nucleus.
Why did it not work?	**11.** Theory did not work for elements other than _____.

☾ *Atomic Mass, Atomic Number, and Isotopes*

Each element has a specific number of protons in its nucleus. This is known as the element's *atomic number*. Most of the mass of the atom is found in the nucleus. Therefore, the mass of an atom is based on the number of protons and neutrons in the nucleus. The total number of protons and neutrons in an atom's nucleus is the *mass number*. While the number of protons for an element is always the same for that element, the number of neutrons can vary. Atoms with the same number of protons, but a different number of neutrons are called *isotopes*.

Scientists write out isotopes using the element's symbol, atomic number, and mass number. Below are the symbols for the two isotopes of Chlorine:

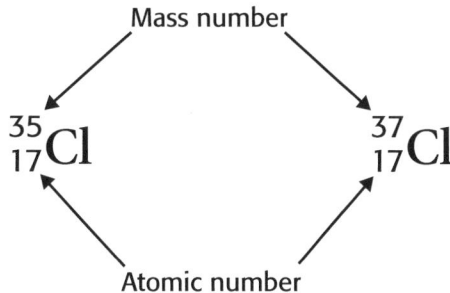

	Chlorine-35	Chlorine-37
Protons	17	17
Neutrons	18	20
Electrons	17	17

The table below lists the isotope symbols for many different atoms. Complete the table by filling in the missing data.

Isotope	Name	Atomic Number	Protons	Neutrons	Mass Number
$^{64}_{30}$Zn	Zinc-64	**1.**	**2.**	34	64
3.	Silver-107	47	**4.**	**5.**	**6.**
$^{41}_{19}$K	**7.**	**8.**	**9.**	22	**10.**
$^{22}_{10}$Ne	**11.** Neon-_____	10	10	**12.**	22

The Periodic Table

Elements are organized in the periodic table. Identify the metals, metalloids, nonmetals, and noble gases on the periodic table.

Periodic Table of the Elements

Legend	
□ Alkali Metals	⊞ Actinide series
■ Alkaline earth metals	▣ Metalloids
▣ Transition metals	▣ Nonmetals
□ Lanthanide series	■ Noble gasses

C Solid
Br Liquid
H Gas
Tc Synthetic

Atomic number — 13
Element symbol — Al
Element name — Aluminum
Average atomic mass — 26.981

1 IA																		18 VIIIA
1 H Hydrogen 1.00794	2 IIA											13 IIIA	14 IVA	15 VA	16 VIA	17 VIIA		2 He Helium 4.002
3 Li Lithium 6.941	4 Be Beryllium 9.012												5 B Boron 10.811	6 C Carbon 12.010	7 N Nitrogen 14.006	8 O Oxygen 15.999	9 F Fluorine 18.998	10 Ne Neon 20.179
11 Na Sodium 22.989	12 Mg Magnesium 24.305	3 IIIB	4 IVB	5 VB	6 VIB	7 VIIB	8	9 VIIIB	10	11 IB	12 IIB	13 Al Aluminum 26.981	14 Si Silicone 28.085	15 P Phosphorus 30.973	16 S Sulfur 32.066	17 Cl Chlorine 35.453	18 Ar Argon 39.948
19 K Potassium 39.098	20 Ca Calcium 40.078	21 Sc Scandium 44.995	22 Ti Titanium 47.867	23 V Vandium 50.941	24 Cr Chromium 51.996	25 Mn Manganese 54.938	26 Fe Iron 55.845	27 Co Cobalt 58.933	28 Ni Nickel 58.693	29 Cu Copper 63.546	30 Zn Zinc 65.409	31 Ga Gallium 69.723	32 Ge Germanium 72.64	33 As Arsenic 74.921	34 Se Selenium 78.96	35 Br Bromine 79.904	36 Kr Krypton 83.798
37 Rb Rubidium 85.467	38 Sr Strontium 87.62	39 Y Yttrium 87.62	40 Zr Zirconium 91.224	41 Nb Niobium 92.906	42 Mo Molybdenum 95.94	43 Tc Technetium 98	44 Ru Ruthenium 101.07	45 Rh Rhodium 102.905	46 Pd Palladium 106.42	47 Ag Silver 107.868	48 Cd Cadmium 112.411	49 In Indium 114.818	50 Sn Tin 118.710	51 Sb Antimony 121.760	52 Te Tellurium 127.60	53 I Iodine 126.904	54 Xe Xenon 131.293
55 Cs Cesium 132.905	56 Ba Barium 137.327		72 Hf Hafnium 178.49	73 Ta Tantalum 180.947	74 W Tungsten 183.84	75 Re Rhenium 186.207	76 Os Osmium 190.23	77 Ir Indium 192.217	78 Pt Platinum 195.078	79 Au Gold 196.966	80 Hg Mercury 200.59	81 Tl Thallium 204.383	82 Pb Lead 207.2	83 Bi Bismuth 208.980	84 Po Polonium 209	85 At Astatine 210	86 Rn Radon 222
87 Fr Francium 223	88 Ra Radium 226		104 Rf Rutherfordium 261	105 Db Dubnium 262	106 Sg Seabargium 266	107 Bh Bohrium 264	108 Hs Hassium 269	109 Mt Meitnerium 268	110 Ds Darmstadtium 271	111 Rg Roentgenium 272	112 Uub Ununbium 285	113 Uut Ununtrium 284	114 Uuq Ununquadium 289	115 Uup Ununpentium 288	116 Uuh Ununhexium 292		

57 La Lanthanum 138.905	58 Ce Cerium 140.116	59 Pr Praseodymium 140.907	60 Nd Neodymium 144.24	61 Pm Promethium 145	62 Sm Samarium 150.36	63 Eu Europium 151.964	64 Gd Gadolinium 157.25	65 Tb Terbium 158.925	66 Dy Dysprosium 162.500	67 Ho Holmium 164.930	68 Er Erbium 167.259	69 Tm Thulium 168.934	70 Yb Ytterbium 173.04	71 Lu Lutetium 174.967
89 Ac Actinium 227	90 Th Thorium 232.038	91 Pa Protactinium 231.035	92 U Uranium 238.028	93 Np Neptunium 237	94 Pu Plutonium 244	95 Am Americium 243	96 Cm Curium 247	97 Bk Berkelium 247	98 Cf Californium 251	99 Es Einsteinium 252	100 Fm Fermium 257	101 Md Mendelevium 258	102 No Nobelium 259	103 Lr Lawrencium 262

Circle the term in each pair of terms that makes each statement below true.

1. Most of the elements in the periodic table are classified as [metals / non-metals].

2. Beryllium, magnesium, and calcium are members of the same [group / period].

3. According to the periodic table, the atomic mass of sodium is [11 / 22.99].

4. Elements found on the right side of the periodic table are [metals / non-metals].

5. Sodium, boron, and fluorine are part of the same [group / period].

6. Chlorine, fluorine, and bromine have similar chemical properties as does [iodine / oxygen].

7. The atomic number of iron is [26 / 55.85].

8. There are [six / eight] elements in Group 2 of the periodic table.

9. Groups 3 through 12 are known as the [alkali / transition] metals.

10. Most of the elements that are actinides are [made in laboratories / naturally occurring] and are [radioactive / stable].

11. Cadmium has [48 / 112] protons in its nucleus.

Periodic Trends

Many of the properties of elements tend to change in a regular fashion. These regular changes happen as you move across a period or down a group.

Explore how the property of atomic size, also known as the atomic radius, varies across a period. Use the data in the table to answer the questions that follow.

Element	Period	Atomic Number	Atomic Radius (picometers)
Lithium	2	3	152
Beryllium	2	4	112
Boron	2	5	85
Carbon	2	6	77
Nitrogen	2	7	75
Oxygen	2	8	73
Flourine	2	9	72
Neon	2	10	71
Sodium	3	11	186
Magnesium	3	12	160
Aluminum	3	13	143
Silicon	3	14	118
Phosphorus	3	15	110
Sulfur	3	16	103
Chlorine	3	17	100
Argon	3	18	98

For each statement below, circle the term in each pair that makes the statement true.

1. Compare the atomic radius of lithium and beryllium. As the atomic number [decreases / increases] the atomic radius [decreases / increases].

2. Compare the atomic radii across the rest of Period 2 (elements beryllium to neon). Across this period (from left to right) as the atomic number [decreases / increases] the atomic radius [decreases / increases].

3. Compare the atomic radii across Period 3 (sodium to argon). Across this period (from left to right) as the atomic number [decreases / increases] the atomic radius [decreases / increases].

4. Lithium and sodium are in the same group on the periodic table (Group 1A). Compare their radii going down the group (from top to bottom). As the atomic number [decreases / increases] the atomic radius [decreases / increases].

☾ Metals, Nonmetals, and Metalloids

Elements are classified as metals, nonmetals, and metalloids (or semi metals). Complete the table below comparing these classes of elements.

Type	Metals	Nonmetals	Metalloids
Physical Properties	**1.** Shiny or have _____	**2.** _____ color	**3.** Usually _____ color
	4. _____ conductor of electricity	**5.** _____ conductor of electricity	**6.** _____ conductor of electricity
	7. Can be _____ into thin sheets and drawn into a _____	N/A	N/A
	Most are solids	Most are gases If solid, they are brittle	**8.** Most are _____
Chemical Properties	**9.** Some are reactive and form _____ compounds; some are _____	**10.** Readily form _____ covalent compounds, except Group _____ elements	**11.** Most form _____ compounds
Location on the Periodic Table	**12.** _____ and middle of the table	**13.** _____ side of the table	**14.** Elements on both sides _____ line on the table

Classify each statement as describing a metal, nonmetal, or metalloid. Write *Me* in the blank if the statement describes a metal, *Md* if the statement describes a metalloid, and *N* if the statement describes a nonmetal.

15. _____ These elements are ductile (can be drawn into a wire) and malleable (hammered into shape).

16. _____ Included in this category are the noble gases.

17. _____ The element silicon.

18. _____ Elements in this category are used to make computer chips.

19. _____ Many of the elements in this category have low boiling points, meaning they are gases at room temperature.

20. _____ Some elements in this category can be made into magnets.

21. _____ Groups 1A and 2A are elements in this category.

Physical Science • © Saddleback Educational Publishing • www.sdlback.com

Lewis/Electron Dot Structures

The chemical properties of an element are determined by the electrons in the outer most energy level. These electrons are called *valence electrons.*

Below is the data for oxygen and its Lewis Structure.

Oxygen	
Atomic Number	8
Electrons	
1st energy level	2
2nd energy level	6
Number of valence electrons	6

Rules for Lewis Structures

- Find the total number of electrons—the atomic number equals the total number of electrons.
- Distribute the electrons to the energy levels, starting with the first energy level.
- The last energy level with electrons has the valence electrons.
- Place a dot for each valence electron around the element's symbol. One dot is placed in each side, and then pair up the electrons.
- There can be no more than 8 dots (valence electrons).

Complete the table below, including a Lewis Structure for each atom.

Element	Atomic Number	Electrons	Valence Electrons	Lewis Structure
Sodium	11	1st: 2 2nd: 8 3rd: 1	1	Na·
Aluminum	13	1st: 2 2nd: 8 3rd: 3	1.	2.
Argon	18	1st: 2 2nd: 8 3rd: 8	3.	4.
Chlorine	17	1st: 2 2nd: 8 3rd: 7	5.	6.
Silicon	14	1st: 2 2nd: 8 3rd: 4	7.	8.

Ionic Bonds

An *ionic bond* forms when atoms exchange valence electrons. In most ionic bonds, one atom loses valence electrons while another adds electrons to its outer most energy level. The example below shows ionic bonding between potassium and fluorine using Lewis structures.

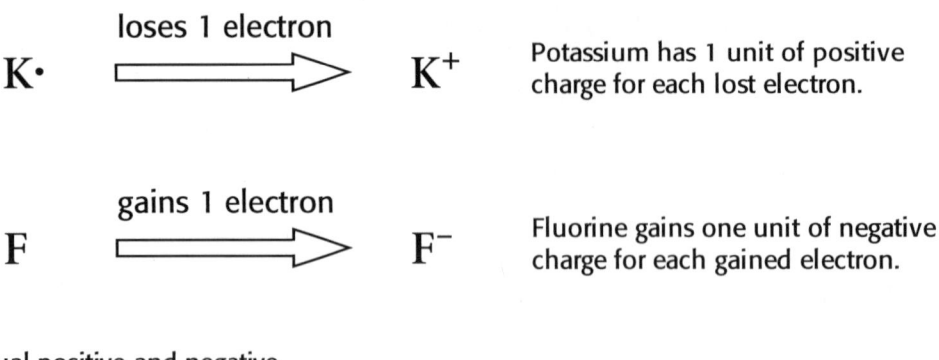

K· $\xrightarrow{\text{loses 1 electron}}$ K$^+$ Potassium has 1 unit of positive charge for each lost electron.

F $\xrightarrow{\text{gains 1 electron}}$ F$^-$ Fluorine gains one unit of negative charge for each gained electron.

Equal positive and negative charges attract.   KF

Explore ionic bonding by completing the table below. Remember the rules for forming ionic bonds and compounds.

- An atom element with 1, 2, or 3 valence electrons will usually lose all valence electrons.
- An atom/element with 5, 6, or 7 valence electrons will gain enough electrons to achieve 8 valence electrons.
- The total amount in the ionic compound of positive charge must equal the total negative charge.

Elements	Number of Electrons Lost or Gained	Ion	Compound
Mg Cl	2 lost 1 gained	Mg^{2+} 2 Cl$^-$	MgCl$_2$
Ca O	1. 3.	2. 4.	5.
Na S	6. 8.	7. 9.	10.
H Cl	11. 13.	12. 14.	15.

Formulas and Names of Ionic Compounds

The combining of positive and negative ions forms *ionic compounds*. When an ionic compound forms, the total positive charge must equal the total negative charge. One way to do this is to switch the number of the charge, making it a subscript for the other ion. Remember, a subscript is a number below and to the right of the symbol indicating the number of atoms in the compound.

> **Example:**
> What is the formula for Aluminum oxide?
> Al^{3+} O^{2-} Al_2O_3
> Check to see if the charges balance:
> Al^{3+}: (2 ions × 3+) = 6+
> O^{2-}: (3 ions × 2–) = 6–

Common Ions	
Positive Ions	
Lithium	Li^+
Sodium	Na^+
Potassium	K^+
Calcium	Ca^{2+}
Magnesium	Mg^{2+}
Aluminum	Al^{3+}
Negative Ions	
Fluoride	F^-
Chloride	Cl^-
Iodide	I^-
Oxide	O^{2-}
Sulfide	S^{2-}
Nitrate	$(NO_3)^-$
Sulfate	$(SO_4)^{2-}$
Carbonate	$(CO_3)^{2-}$

Use the table to the right to determine the formula for each ionic compound.

Compound	Formula
Lithium chloride	1.
Magnesium floride	2.
Calcium carbonate	3.
Potassium oxide	4.
Aluminum nitrate	5.

To name an ionic compound made of at least two elements, follow the rules below. Use the the rules to help you name the following compounds.

Rules for naming ionic compounds.
- Identify the positive and negative ions in the compound. The positive ion is the first element.
- The second element is the negative ion.
- The name of the positive ion remains unchanged; the last part of the name of the negative ion is dropped and replaced with "ide."

Compound	Positive Ion	Negative Ion		Name
KCl	potassium	chlorine ⇒ chloride		potassium chloride
BeO	6.	7. _____ ⇒ _____		8.
CaF_2	9.	10. _____ ⇒ _____		11.

☾ *Covalent Bonds*

When atoms combine chemically, rather than gain or lose electrons, the atoms form a chemical bond by sharing electrons. This type of chemical bond is known as a covalent bond.

How does a chlorine atom bond with another chlorine atom? For each set of atoms, complete the diagram showing the covalent bond or bonds.

Step 1 Show each atom with its Lewis structure.

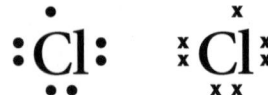

Step 2 Count the number of valence electrons.

Each atom has **1.** _____ valence electrons.

Step 3 How many electrons are needed to have 8 valence electrons?

Each atom needs 1 electron to get to 8.

Step 4 Move the Lewis structures together so one "electron" from each atom is in between each atom.

Shared pair of electrons

Step 5 Count the number of electrons for each atom.

The electrons in the middle count for each atom, so each now has 8.

For each set of atoms, complete the diagram showing the covalent bond or bonds.

Fluorine (F$_2$)	2.	3.
Water (H$_2$O)	4.	5.
Methane (CH$_4$)	6.	7.

Physical Science • © Saddleback Educational Publishing • www.sdlback.com

Double and Triple Covalent Bonds

In many covalent compounds, atoms sharing more than one pair of electrons form the molecule. When atoms share more than one pair of electrons they form a *double* or *triple covalent bond.* As with a simple single covalent bond each atom in the compound needs to have eight (8) electrons through the bonding.

How do two oxygen atoms bond?

Step 1 Write the Lewis structure for each atom—each oxygen has 6 valence electrons.

Step 2 Pair up electrons that are shown as single electrons.

Step 3 Count up the electrons with each atom.

Each oxygen has 7 electrons—they share 2 electrons.

Step 4 Continue to pair up lone electrons—move lone electrons in between the atoms.

Each oxygen is sharing 2 pairs of electrons in double pairs

How do two nitrogen atoms combine?

Step 1 Write the Lewis structure for each atom—each nitrogen has 5 valence electrons.

Step 2 Pair up electrons that are shown as single electrons.

Step 3 Count up the electrons with each atom.

Each nitrogen has 5 electrons—they share 2 electrons.

Step 4 Continue to pair up lone electrons—move lone electrons in between the atoms.

Each nitrogen is sharing 3 pairs of electrons in double pairs

Use Lewis structures to diagram the bonding in the following molecules.

1. CO_2 O   C   O

2. C_2H_2 H   C   C   H

3. CS_2 S   C   S

Names of Covalent Compounds

Part of the name of a covalent compound is a prefix telling you the number of atoms of each element in the compound.

Naming covalent compounds made of two different elements follows some basic rules.

Rules for naming covalent compounds made of two elements.

- The first element in the formula is named first, using the entire element name.
- The second element drops the last part of its name and adds the ending "ide."
- Prefixes are used to tell the number of atoms of each element.

Number of Atoms	Prefix
1	**1.**
2.	di
3	**3.**
4	**4.**
5.	penta
6	**6.**
7.	hepta
8	**8.**
9.	nona
10	**10.**

Complete the table to the right summarizing the prefixes used in covalent compounds.

Name the compound P$_2$O$_5$.

Compound	Element Name	Number of Atoms	Prefixes	Compound Name
P$_2$O$_5$	Phosphorus	2	**11.** _____ and _____	Diphosphorus pentoxide
	Oxygen (Oxide)	5		

Name each of the following compounds. (Use the table above.)

Compound	Element Name	Number of Atoms	Prefixes	Compound Name
CF$_4$	**12.**	**13.**	**14.**	**15.**
As$_2$O$_3$	**16.**	**17.**	**18.**	**19.**
NO$_3$	**20.**	**21.**	**22.**	**23.**
NF$_3$	**24.**	**25.**	**26.**	**27.**
S$_4$N$_4$	**28.**	**29.**	**30.**	**31.**
SeO$_2$	**32.**	**33.**	**34.**	**35.**

Physical Science • © Saddleback Educational Publishing • www.sdlback.com

(Mass of a Compound

The mass of a compound is equal to the mass of every particle making up the compound. With the help of the periodic table you can find the mass of any compound.

What is the mass of the compound potassium chromate (K_2CrO_4)?

Compound	Elements	Number of Atoms	Mass of Atoms	Total
K_2CrO_4	K Cr O	2 1 4	39.1 52.0 16.0	78.2 52.0 64.0
			Total mass	194.2

If you are measuring the mass of one formula unit (for an ionic compound) or one molecule (for a covalent compound), then the mass of the substance is in atomic mass units (amu). If you are measuring the mass of a quantity known as a mole, the mass of a compound is in grams.

Determine the mass of the following compounds:

Compound	Elements	Number of Atoms	Mass of Atoms	Total
NaOH	Na O H	**1.** **2.** **3.**	**4.** **5.** **6.**	**7.** **8.** **9.**
			Total mass	**10.**
$MgCl_2$	Mg Cl	**11.** **12.**	**13.** **14.**	**15.** **16.**
			Total mass	**17.**
$C_6H_{12}O_6$	C H O	**18.** **19.** **20.**	**21.** **22.** **23.**	**24.** **25.** **26.**
			Total mass	**27.**

Balancing Chemical Equations

According to the laws of conservation of matter, during a chemical reaction the mass of the reactants equals the mass of the products. At an atomic level, this law means that the number of atoms of each element present before the reaction must equal the number of atoms of each element after the reaction occurs and the products are formed.

Balance the following equation: $Mg + O_2 \rightarrow MgO$.

Step 1 You can represent the equation with symbols or individual atoms.

$$Mg + O_2 \rightarrow MgO$$
or
$$Mg + O\text{–}O \rightarrow MgO$$

Step 2 List each element and count the number of atoms of each element on each side of the arrow.

$$Mg + O_2 \rightarrow MgO$$

1	Mg	1
2	O	1

Step 3 Place numbers in front of the formulas (called coefficients).

$$2Mg + O_2 \rightarrow 2MgO$$

1	Mg	1
2	O	1

$$2Mg + O_2 \rightarrow 2MgO$$

Balance the following equations:

1. $H_2 + N_2 \rightarrow NH_3$

2. $H_2 + O_2 \rightarrow H_2O$

3. $Al_2O_3 \rightarrow Al + O_2$

4. $SO_2 + O_2 \rightarrow SO_3$

5. $Fe + HCl \rightarrow FeCl_2 + H_2$

Physical Science • © Saddleback Educational Publishing • www.sdlback.com

Classifying Chemical Reactions

Chemical reactions are classified by what happens in the reaction to the reactants and the products. The four types of reactions are listed below.

Explore the types of chemical reactions by completing the table below.

Type	Description
Synthesis Reaction A + X → AX	**1.** Two or more substances combine to form _____. $2Hg + O_2 \rightarrow 2HgO$
Decomposition Reaction AX → A + X	**2.** _____ breaks down into two or more substances. $2H_2O \rightarrow 2H_2 + O_2$
Single Replacement Reaction A + BX → AX + B	**3.** One _____ replaces another element in a compound. $Fe + 2HCl \rightarrow FeCl_2 + H_2$
Double Replacement Reaction AX + BY → AY + BX	**4.** Two elements in different _____ replace each other. $HCl + NaOH \rightarrow H_2O + NaCl$

Classify each of the following reactions as synthesis, decomposition, single replacement, or double replacement.

5. _____ $3H_2 + N_2 \rightarrow 2NH_3$

6. _____ $CaCO_3 + 2HCl \rightarrow CaCl_2 + H_2CO_3$

7. _____ $2SO_2 + O_2 + 2H_2O \rightarrow 2H_2SO_4$

8. _____ $2H_2O_2 \rightarrow 2H_2O + O_2$

9. _____ $2Al + Fe_2O_3 \rightarrow Al_2O_3 + 2Fe$

10. _____ $P_4O_{10} + 6H_2O \rightarrow 4H_3PO_4$

11. _____ $Zn + 2HCl \rightarrow ZnCl_2 + H_2$

12. _____ $CuO + H_2SO_4 \rightarrow CuSO_4 + H_2O$

Exothermic and Endothermic Reactions

During a chemical reaction energy is either released or absorbed. The graphs below show the relative energy changes involved in each type of reaction.

Compare an exothermic and endothermic reaction by completing the graphs.

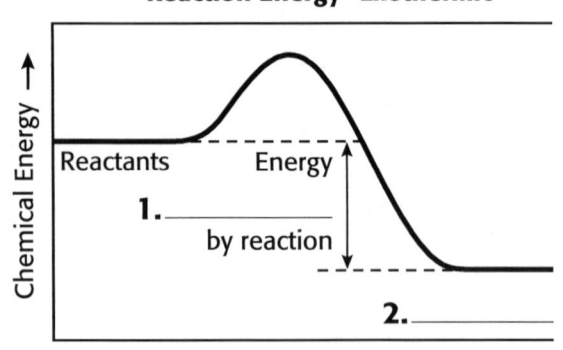

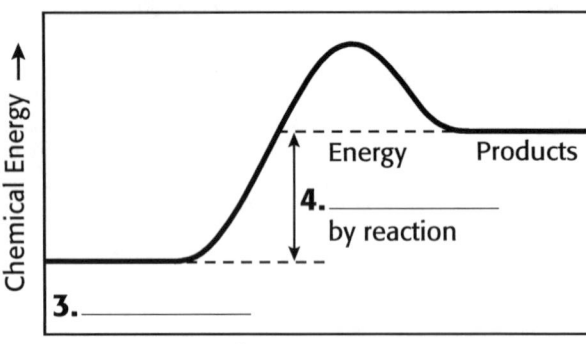

Classify each statement as referring to an exothermic or endothermic reaction. Write *Exo* if the statement refers to an exothermic reaction, *Endo* if the statement refers to an endothermic reaction, or *Both* if the statement refers to both types of reactions.

5. _____ A chemical reaction that absorbs energy from its surroundings.

6. _____ More energy is required to break the bonds in the reactants than is released by the forming of the products.

7. _____ Consider the reaction below:
$CaO + H_2O \rightarrow Ca(OH)_2 + 65.2$ kJ
Is this reaction exothermic or endothermic?

8. _____ Follows the law of conservation of energy: the total amount of energy before the reaction is equal to the total amount of energy after the reaction.

9. _____ A reaction that releases energy to its surroundings.

10. _____ Consider the reaction below:
$2NaHCO_3 + 129$ kJ $\rightarrow Na_2CO_3 + H_2O + CO_2$
Is this reaction exothermic or endothermic?

11. _____ The energy released on the products forming is greater than the energy needed to break the bonds in the reactants.

12. _____ Energy is needed by the reactants to break the bonds in the reactants for the reaction to proceed.

13. _____ The chemical energy of the reactants is greater than the chemical energy of the products.

Physical Science • © Saddleback Educational Publishing • www.sdlback.com

Chemical Equilibrium

Not all chemical reactions result in all the reactants being used and only products being present. Many reactions are reversible—reactants interact to form products and products interact to reform the reactants. In a closed system chemical equilibrium is established, reactants change into products, and just as fast, products change back into reactants.

Changes in Concentrations of Reactants and Products

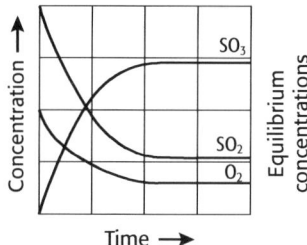

Use the graph above to explore the nature of chemical equilibrium. Circle the term in each pair that makes the statement true.

1. At the beginning of the reaction the reactants are sulfur dioxide (SO_2) and [oxygen (O_2) / sulfur trioxide (SO_3)].

2. The product of the reaction is [oxygen (O_2) / sulfur trioxide (SO_3)].

3. The amounts of each substance present at equilibrium are found on the [left / right] side of the graph.

4. The least abundant gas at equilibrium is [oxygen (O_2) / sulfur trioxide (SO_3)].

5. Once equilibrium is reached, the amounts of reactants and products will [continue to change / stay the same].

Several factors will affect a chemical system's equilibrium. Explore the nature of these factors by completing the table below.

Factor	Increase	Decrease
Temperature	**6.** Shifts in the direction that _____ heat	**7.** Shifts in the direction that would _____ heat
Pressure	**8.** Shifts in the direction that _____ pressure or _____ gas molecules	**9.** Shifts in the direction that _____ pressure or a _____ number of gas molecules
Amount of a substance	**10.** Shifts in the direction that _____ the added substance	**11.** Shifts in the direction that _____ the removed substance

Solutions

Explain the nature of solutions by labeling each statement as true or false. Place a *T* in the space if the statement is true. Place an *F* in the space if the statement is false. For each false statement, replace the underlined word with one that will make the statement true.

1. _____ In a solution, the material that does the dissolving, or the material in a greater

   amount, is the solvent. _____

2. _____ Air is an example of a gas-solid solution, with nitrogen as the solvent. _____

3. _____ Salt is dissolved in water. The freezing point of water as a result increases.

   _____

4. _____ Sugar dissolves in water by dispersion, the breaking of a solute into small pieces

   that spread throughout the water. _____

5. _____ In a solution, the material that is dissolved, or is present in the lower amount,

   is the solute. _____

6. _____ Breaking a solute into smaller pieces decreases the rate at which a substance

   dissolves. _____

Several factors affect if or how much of a solvent used dissolves in a solution. Complete the table below determining if a solution is possible.

Solvent	Solute	Solution Likely
Polar	Polar/ionic	7.
Polar	8.	No
Nonpolar	9.	No
10.	Nonpolar	Yes

Complete each statement by circling the term in each pair that makes the statement true.

11. A solvent dissolves a solute only if the solvent and solute are [alike / different].

12. An increase in pressure over a solution will [decrease / increase] the solubility of a gas.

13. Oil is a nonpolar substance. Water is a polar substance. Oil [will / will not] dissolve in water.

Physical Science • © Saddleback Educational Publishing • www.sdlback.com

Solubility Curves

The amount of a substance that can dissolve into a solution depends on several factors, including temperature.

Use the data in the table below to graph the solubility of potassium nitrate in water. Be sure to connect your data points with a smooth curve or straight line.

Temperature (°C)	Solubility in 1,000 g H_2O
0	13 g
20	31 g
40	65 g
60	108 g
80	164 g
100	247 g

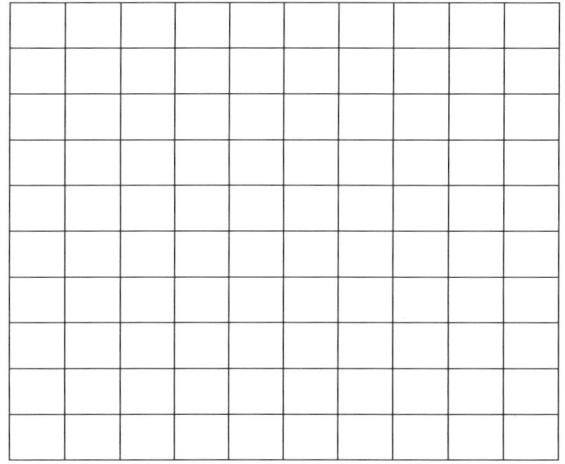

Use the data in the table and the graph to complete each statement.

1. In general, as the temperature increases the solubility will _____.

2. Suppose you had 100 g of water at 120°C. How much potassium nitrate do you think you could dissolve?

3. Based on the graph and data, you should be able to dissolve 50 g of potassium nitrate at about _____°C.

4. Based on the graph and data table, you could dissolve _____ g of potassium nitrate at 50°C.

5. Ammonia (NH_3) is a gas. Look at the graph and complete the following statement regarding the solubility of a gas: The solubility of a gas _____ as the temperature of the solution increases.

6. The compound _____ is the least soluble at 0°C.

7. The compound _____ has the greatest solubility at 0°C.

Comparing Acids and Bases

Compare the properties of acids and bases by completing the table below.

Property	Acid	Base
Taste	**1.**	**2.**
Feel	N/A	**3.**
Reactivity with some metals	**4.** Reacts to form _____	**5.** _____ react with metals
Reaction with some carbonates (such as baking soda)	**6.** Reacts to form _____	Does not react with carbonates
Litmus paper test	**7.** Red litmus turns _____	**8.** Blue litmus turns _____
Conducts electricity?	**9.**	**10.**
Ion produced in water solution	**11.**	**12.**
Examples	HCl HNO$_3$	NaOH KOH

Explore the nature of acids and bases by classifying each statement as referring to an acid or a base. Place an *A* in the blank if the statement refers to an acid, or a *B* if it refers to a base.

13. _____ The solution H$_2$SO$_4$ is found in a car's battery.

14. _____ Soap is made with NaOH.

15. _____ Antacids are often made with a compound that has a hydroxide group to neutralize the excess acid in the stomach.

16. _____ The sour taste of lemons is due to this class of compounds.

17. _____ Litmus paper turns pink when dipped in vinegar.

18. _____ Look at the reaction below:
Zn + 2HCl → H$_2$ + 2ZnCl$_2$
Based on the reaction, HCl belongs to this class of compounds.

Strength of Acids and Bases

Not every acid is a strong acid, nor is every base a strong base. For each statement below, write *SA* in the blank if the statement refers to a strong acid, *SB* if it refers to a strong base, *WA* if it refers to a weak acid, or *WB* if it refers to a weak base.

1. _____ Acetic acid ionizes only slightly in water.

2. _____ The dissolving of calcium hydroxide ($Ca(OH)_2$) favors the products of the solution process because the ions do not tend to recombine.

3. _____ The reaction below shows which type of solution?
$NH_3 + H_2O \rightarrow NH_4^+ + OH^-$

4. _____ When hydrogen chloride (HCl) dissolves in water, almost all of its molecules ionize.

5. _____ The reaction below shows which type of solution?
$HNO_3 + H_2O \rightarrow H_3O^+ + NO_3^-$

One way to describe an acid or base solution is to describe the concentration of hydronium ions (H_3O^+) in solution. For each statement below, write *A* in the blank if the statement refers to an acid solution, a *B* if the statement refers to a base solution, and an *N* if the statement refers to a neutral solution.

6. _____ A solution has a pH of 1.

7. _____ Drain cleaner has a pH of 13.5.

8. _____ Water has a pH of 7.

9. _____ A solution has more hydronium ions (H_3O^+) in solution than hydroxide ions (OH^-).

10. _____ Baking soda dissolved in water has a pH of about 8.5.

11. The table to the right lists the pH of several common items.

List the items in order from most acidic to most basic.

_____

_____

_____

_____

Substance	pH
Ammonia	11.5
Blood	7.5
Lemon juice	2.2
Milk	6.3
Seawater	8.5
Stomach acid	1.7
Tomato juice	4.1

Naming Acids and Bases

Acids are substances that produce hydrogen ions (H^+) in a water solution. There are two types of acids, acids made of two elements and acids made of more than two elements, one element being oxygen.

You can use the following rules for naming an acid:

- Examine the formula; if there are only two elements, then go to 2; if there are three elements go to 3.
- The first part of the name is "hydro."
  The second part of the acid name is the root of the second element plus "ic."
- Use the root of the element that is *not* hydrogen or oxygen.
  If the negative ion ends in "ite," then the acid ends "ous acid."
      H_2SO_{3-} ⇒ Sulfurous acid
  If the negative ion ends in "ate," then the acid ends in "ic acid."
      H_2SO_{4-} ⇒ Sulfuric Acid

Name the acid HI and H_3PO_4.

	HI	H_3PO_4
Is the acid made of two or more than two elements?	2	3
What is the first part of the name of the acid?	"hydro"	"phosphor"
What is the second part of the same acid?	"iodic acid"	"ic acid"
Combine the two parts.	hydroiodic acid	phosphoric acid

Name the following acids:

	HF	HCl	H_3PO_3	HNO_3
Is the acid made of two or more than two elements?	1.	2.	3.	4.
What is the first part of the name of the acid?	5.	6.	7.	8.
What is the second part of the same acid?	9.	10.	11.	12.
Combine the two parts.	13.	14.	15.	16.

Physical Science • © Saddleback Educational Publishing • www.sdlback.com

Neutralization and Salts

There are times when your stomach produces too much acid. To get rid of the excess, you can take an antacid. The antacid neutralizes the excess acid. The equation below demonstrates such a reaction.

$$2HCl + Mg(OH)_2 \rightarrow MgCl_2 + 2H_2O$$

Use the equation above to explore the nature of a neutralization reaction. For each statement, circle the term in each pair that makes the statement true.

1. A neutralization reaction is a chemical reaction in which a(n) [acid / salt] and [a base / water] reacts to form a(n) [acid / salt] and [a base / water].

2. In the reaction above, the acid is [HCl / $Mg(OH)_2$].

3. In the reaction above, the base is [HCl / $Mg(OH)_2$].

4. In the reaction above, the salt is [HCl / $MgCl_2$].

5. A salt is a(n) [covalent / ionic] compound that forms when an acid reacts with a base.

6. To form the salt NaCl (sodium chloride) you could react the base [$MgCl_2$ / NaOH] with the acid [HCl / $MgCl_2$].

7. In forming salt from a neutralization reaction, the positive ion in the salt comes from the [acid / base] and the negative ion of the reaction comes from the [acid / base].

For each salt, select the acid and base that will produce the salt in a neutralization reaction.

Acid	Base	Salt
8.	**9.**	Na_2CO_3 sodium carbonate
10.	**11.**	KCl potassium chloride
12.	**13.**	$MgBr_2$ magnesium bromide

Hydrocarbons

There are several types of hydrocarbons—compounds made of hydrogen and carbon. The different types are classified by whether they form a straight chain or a ring plus the number of covalent bonds between carbon atoms.

Compare the types of hydrocarbons by completing the table below.

Type	General Formula	Carbon-Carbon Bonds	Example	Structural Formula
Alkane	$C_{(n)}H_{(2n+2)}$	**1.**	**2.**	H–C–C–H
Alkene	**3.**	double	C_2H_4–ethene	**4.**
Alkyne	C_nH_n	**5.**	C_2H_2–ethyne	**6.**

Properties of Alkanes

The table below shows the boiling point of the first ten straight-chained alkanes. Complete the table by determining the mass of each molecule. Then on a separate piece of paper graph the mass and the boiling point. Use the graph and the data to complete the statements below.

Name	Molecular Formula	Molecular Mass	Boiling Point (°C)
Methane	CH_4	**7.**	−161.0
Ethane	C_2H_6	**8.**	−88.5
Propane	C_3H_8	**9.**	−42.0
Butane	C_4H_{10}	**10.**	0.5
Pentane	C_5H_{12}	**11.**	36.0
Hexane	C_6H_{14}	**12.**	68.7
Heptane	C_7H_{16}	**13.**	98.5
Octane	C_8H_{18}	**14.**	125.6
Nonane	C_9H_{20}	**15.**	150.7
Decane	$C_{10}H_{22}$	**16.**	174.1

17. The compound with the lowest boiling point is _____.

18. The compound with the highest boiling point is _____.

19. Compare the boiling point of methane and ethane. In going from methane to ethane, the molecular mass _____. In going from methane to ethane, the boiling point _____.

Substituted Hydrocarbons

Carbon-containing compounds that are made of carbon, often hydrogen, plus one or more additional elements, are called *substituted hydrocarbons*. There are many categories of substituted hydrocarbons, each identified by its functional group. A functional group is an atom or group of atoms that always react in a certain way.

Compare the different functional groups by completing the table below.

Compound Type	General Formula	Functional Group
Halocarbon	R – X	**1.** X = F, Cl, I or P
Alcohol	R – OH	**2.**
Ether	R – O – R	**3.**
Amine	R – NH_2	**4.**
Aldehyde	O = C^4 – H	**5.**
Carboxylic acid	C – HO = C – OH	**6.**
Ester	O = C – O – R	**7.**
Amide	O = C – N – RH	**8.**
Ketone	OR – C – R	**9.**

Use the table to identify the classification of each compound shown below.

10.
$$H-\overset{\displaystyle H}{\underset{\displaystyle H}{C}}-Cl$$

11.
$$H_2N-C\overset{\displaystyle O}{\underset{\displaystyle NH_2}{}}$$

12. $CH_3 - CH_2 - O - CH_3$

13. $CH_3 - CH_2 - OH$

14. $CH_3 - \overset{\displaystyle O}{\overset{\displaystyle \|}{C}} - CH_3$

15. $CH_3 - \overset{\displaystyle O}{\overset{\displaystyle \|}{C}} - H$

16. $CH_3 - C\overset{\displaystyle O}{\underset{\displaystyle OH}{}}$

17. $CH_3 - \underset{\displaystyle \underset{\displaystyle O}{\|}}{C} - O\ CH_2\ CH_3$

Types of Radioactive Decay

Compare the types of radiation by completing the table below.

Property	Alpha Particles	Beta Particles	Gamma Radiation
Description	**1.** _____ nucleus	**2.**	**3.** High energy _____ radiation
Symbol	**4.**	**5.**	**6.**
Charge	**7.**	**8.**	**9.**
Effect on nucleus	**10.** Mass number decreases by _____, atomic number decreases by _____	**11.** Mass number stays the same, atomic number _____ by 1	**12.**
Penetrating power	**13.** Blocked by _____	**14.** Blocked by _____	**15.** Not completely blocked by _____ or concrete

Each type of radioactive decay changes an element's nucleus. The result of such a change is an atom of a different element. Explore each type of radioactive decay by completing the equations below.

Alpha Decay: mass number decreases by 4, the atomic number decreases by 2.

16. $^{226}_{88}\text{Ra} \quad \rightarrow {}^{4}_{2}\text{He} \quad + {}^{222}_{86}\text{Rn}$

Radium-_____ → alpha particle + _____

17. $^{238}_{92}\text{U} \quad \rightarrow {}^{4}_{2}\text{He} \quad + {}^{234}_{90}\text{Th}$

_____-238 → alpha particle + _____

Beta Decay: mass number does not change, the atomic number increases by 1.

18. $^{131}_{53}\text{I} \quad \rightarrow {}^{0}_{-1}\beta \quad + {}^{131}_{54}\text{Xe}$

Iodine-_____ → beta particle + _____

19. $^{84}_{35}\text{Br} \quad \rightarrow {}^{0}_{-1}\beta \quad + {}^{84}_{36}\text{Kr}$

_____-84 → beta particle + _____

Nuclear Fission and Fusion

Compare nuclear fission and nuclear fusion. For each statement below, write
Fission **if the statement refers to nuclear fission. Write** *Fusion* **if the statement**
refers to nuclear fusion, or *Both* **if the statement refers to both nuclear fission**
and nuclear fusion.

1. _____ The splitting of an atom's nucleus into smaller parts.

2. _____ Release a large amount of energy as a result of the
nuclear reaction.

3. _____ Look at the nuclear reaction below.
$^{1}_{0}n + ^{236}_{92}U \rightarrow ^{91}_{36}KR + ^{142}_{56}Ba + 3^{1}_{0}n$ + energy
Which type of nuclear reaction is described?

4. _____ The type of nuclear reaction that powers the sun.

5. _____ The type of reaction powering a nuclear power plant.

6. _____ Powers all current nuclear power plants.

7. _____ Look at the nuclear reaction below.
$^{2}_{1}H + ^{2}_{1}H \rightarrow ^{4}_{2}He + ^{1}_{0}n$ + energy
Which type of nuclear reaction is described?

The fusion of hydrogen atoms is the main source of energy for the Sun
(and all stars). Another set of nuclear reactions occurs in stars—the carbon-
nitrogen-oxygen cycle. Explore the cycle by completing the flow chart below.

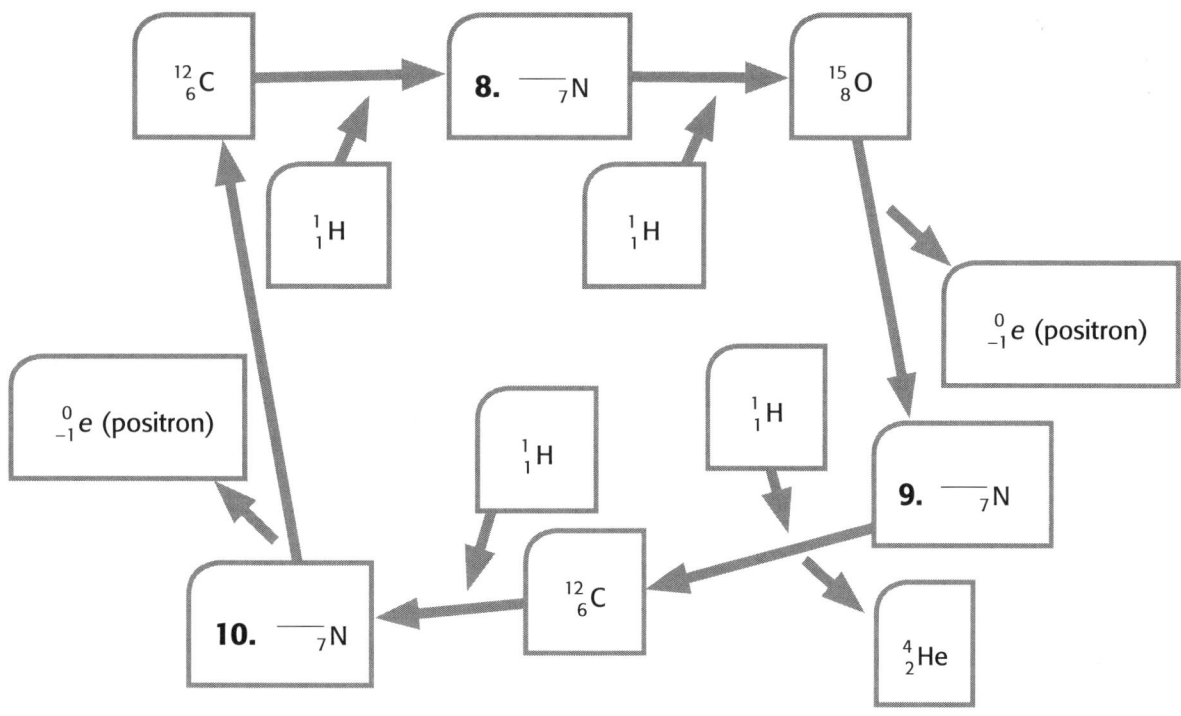

NAME _____   DATE _____

⟨ Half Life

Carbon-14 is a radioactive form of carbon. This form of carbon breaks down into another element and in the process releases radiation. The decay rate for carbon-14 is constant.

Explore the decay of carbon-14 by graphing the carbon-14 and number of years.

	Number of Years	Carbon-14	Decay Product
Start (0)	0	100 g	0.0 g
After 1 half-life	5,730	50 g	50.0 g
After 2nd half-life	11,460	25 g	75.0 g
After 3rd half-life	17,190	12.5 g	87.5 g
After 4th half-life	22,920	6.25 g	93.75 g
After 5th half-life	28,650	3.125 g	96.875 g

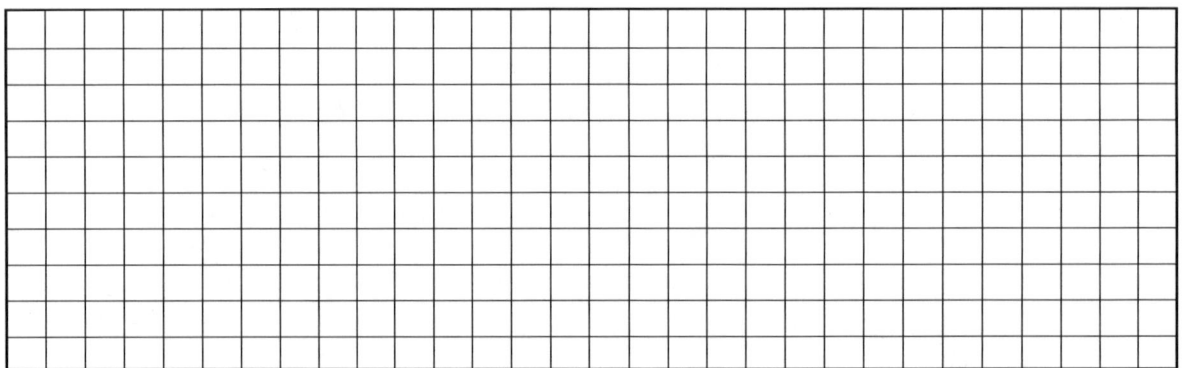

Use the table and graph to help answer the following questions.

1. Half-life is the amount of time it takes for _____ the atom in

a sample to decay.

2. The half-life of Carbon-14 is _____ years.

3. After 2 half lives of Carbon-14, _____ years have passed.

4. You have a fossil that is 20,000 years old. About how many half lives have gone by?

_____

5. In a sample fossil about 10 grams of C-14 remain. The fossil started with 100 grams

of C-14. How old is the fossil? _____

48

Physical Science • © Saddleback Educational Publishing • www.sdlback.com

Decay Series

A radioactive isotope will change to another element through radioactive decay. If the new element is also radioactive, then that isotope will also change to another element through radioactive decay. This process will continue until a non-radioactive isotope results. This set of nuclear reactions is called a *decay series*.

Follow the decay of radon-222 by completing the decay series below.

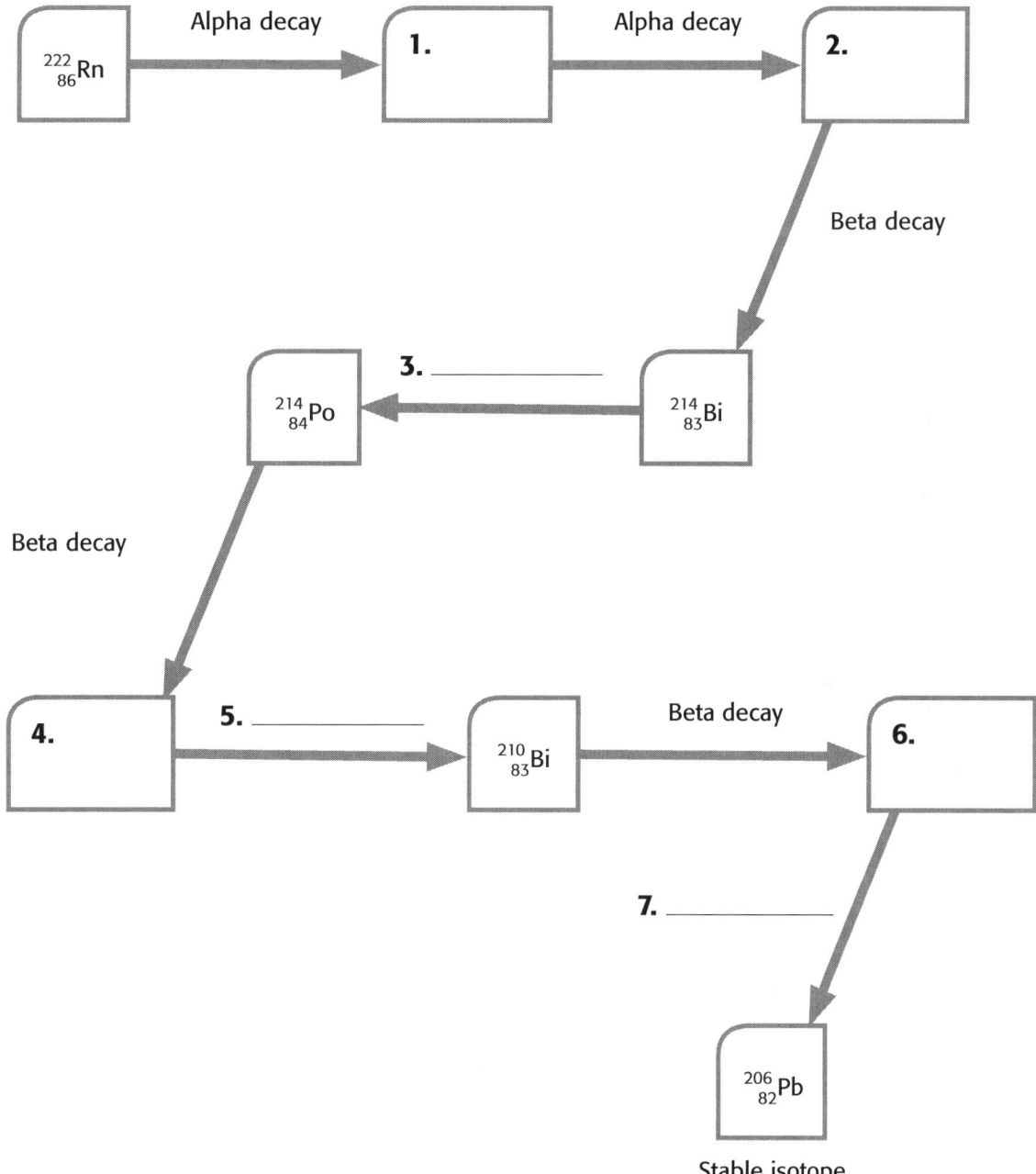

Graphing Motion

Use the data below to graph the motion of an object.

Distance and Time Data	
Time (s)	Distance (m)
0	0
4	200
8	400
12	600
16	800
20	1,000

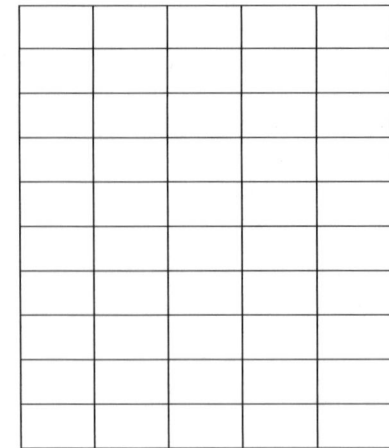

Use the data in the table and the graph. For each item, fill in the blank with the term or terms that will make the statement true.

1. What is the distance traveled between t = 0 s and t = 4 s? _____

2. Is the distance traveled every 4 seconds always the same? _____

3. An object is traveling at a constant speed if the distance traveled over each time interval is the same. Is the object traveling at a constant speed? _____

You can determine the speed of an object if you know the distance traveled and the time it took to travel that distance.

You can use the formula: average speed = $\frac{\text{distance}}{\text{time}}$.

Using the data in the table, calculate the speed of the car between t = 0 s and t = 20 s.

Step 1 What do you know?	t = 0 s and t = 20 s, or time = 20 s
	Distance traveled in that time = 1,000 m
Step 2 What do you need to find?	Speed of the object
Step 3 What formula do you use?	Average speed = $\frac{\text{distance}}{\text{time}}$
Step 4 Use the data in the formula.	Average speed = $\frac{1,000 \text{ m}}{20 \text{ s}}$ = 50 m/s

4. On a trip you travel 240 km in 4 hours. What is the average speed for this part of the trip? _____

Physical Science • © Saddleback Educational Publishing • www.sdlback.com

Acceleration

Acceleration is a change in the speed or direction, or both the speed and direction, of an object. When an object's speed increases, that is *acceleration*. When an object's speed decreases, that too is acceleration.

Use the data in the table below to graph the speed of an object over time.

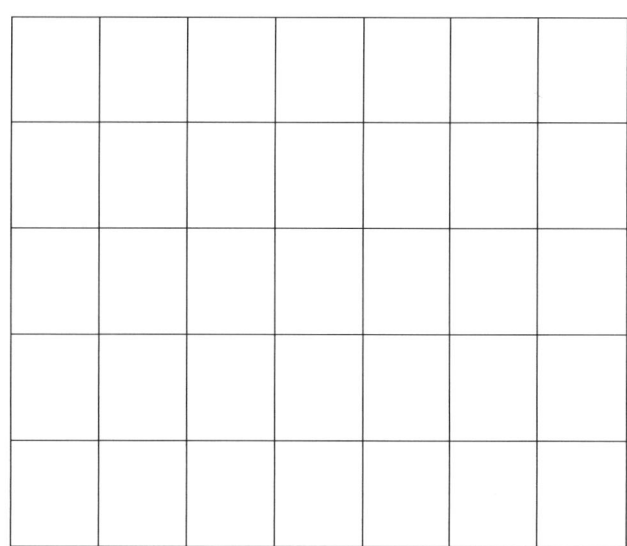

Data for Graph	
Time (s)	Speed (m/s)
0	0
5	10
10	20
15	20
20	20
25	15
30	10
35	5

Use the data and the graph you created from the data. For each statement, fill in the blank with the term that will make each statement true.

1. During the time interval T = 0 to T = 10 the speed of the object is _____.

2. Therefore the acceleration on the object is _____.

3. During the time interval T = 0 to T = 5 the speed goes from _____ m/s to _____ m/s

   or a change in speed of _____ m/s in 5 s. The change in speed from T = 5 to T = 10 is

   _____ m/s in 5 seconds. Therefore, acceleration is _____.

4. During the time interval T = 10 to T = 20 the speed of the object is _____.

5. Therefore, the acceleration is _____.

6. During the time interval T = 20 to T = 35 the speed of the object is _____.

   Therefore, the acceleration is _____.

7. During the time interval T = 20 to T = 25 the speed goes from _____ m/s to _____

   m/s or a change in speed of _____ m/s in 5 s. The change in speed from T = 25 to

   T = 30 is _____ m/s in 5 seconds. Therefore, acceleration is _____.

Balanced and Unbalanced Forces

Explore the nature of balanced and unbalanced forces. Classify each statement as true or false. Place a *T* in the blank if the statement is true. Place an *F* in the blank if the statement is false. If the statement is false, replace the underlined term with a term that makes the statement true.

1. _____ In any situation, the overall force on an object after all the forces are added

   together is called the <u>net force</u>. _____

2. _____ Equal forces acting on an object in opposite directions are called <u>moving</u> forces.

   _____

3. _____ <u>Unbalanced</u> forces acting on an object will not change the object's motion.

   _____

4. _____ A book is resting on a table. Gravity, a force, pulls downward on the book.

   The table exerts a force equal in magnitude and opposite in direction (upward) on

   the book. The forces on the book are <u>balanced</u>. _____

5. _____ A force <u>is needed</u> to keep a moving object moving. _____

6. _____ When you add equal forces exerted in opposite directions, the net force is <u>zero</u>.

   _____

Determine the net force in each of the situations below. For each set of forces, complete the missing parts of the table. Remember force has two parts, direction and magnitude (amount). The longer the arrow, the greater the magnitude of the force.

Forces	F1		F2		Net Force	
	Magnitude	Direction	Magnitude	Direction	Magnitude	Direction
	1	right	**7.**	**8.**	**9.**	**10.**
	11.	**12.**	**13.**	left	0	N/A
	1	right	**14.**	**15.**	**16.**	left
	1	up	**17.**	**18.**	0	N/A
	19.	**20.**	1	down	2	down

Physical Science • © Saddleback Educational Publishing • www.sdlback.com

Newton's First Law of Motion

Explore the nature of Newton's First Law of Motion. For each statement, circle the term from each pair that makes the statement true.

1. Newton's First Law of Motion is often called the law of [inertia / mass].

2. Whether at rest or in motion, every object resists any type of change to its motion. This resistance to a change in motion is called [inertia / mass].

3. According to Newton's first law, unless acted on by a force, an object at rest [remains at rest / can move at anytime].

4. According to Newton's first law of motion, unless acted on by a force, an object in motion at a constant velocity will [continue to move at the same / change] velocity.

5. If no force acts on a moving object, the object will [eventually / not] stop.

6. A ball rolling across a table comes to a stop. The [friction between / mass of] the ball and the table overcomes the natural tendency of the ball to keep moving.

Mass and inertia are related. Classify each statement below as true or false. Place a _T_ in the blank if the statement is true. Place an _F_ in the blank if the statement is false. For each false statement, replace the underlined term with a term that makes the statement true.

7. _____ Volume is the amount of matter in an object. _____

8. _____ Mass is measured in the SI in the unit kilopascals. _____

9. _____ The more mass an object has, the greater the object's inertia. _____

10. _____ Two objects with the same volume will have the same inertia. _____

11. _____ Mass can also be defined as the measure of the motion of an object.

_____

Mass and weight are often considered to be the same thing, but they are not. Place an _M_ in the blank if the statement refers to measuring mass. Place a _W_ in the blank if the statement refers to measuring weight.

12. _____ The measure of the force of gravity on an object.

13. _____ Measured in newtons.

14. _____ The amount of matter in an object.

15. _____ Will be different on Earth and on the Moon.

(Newton's Second Law of Motion

Explore the nature of Newton's Second Law of Motion. For each statement, circle the term in each pair of terms that will make each statement true.

1. According to Newton, a(n) [balanced / unbalanced] force acting on an object will cause a change in the motion of that object.

2. [Acceleration / Inertia] is a change in the motion of an object.

3. A change in the direction in which an object moves is an example of [acceleration / inertia].

4. According to Newton's second law, the acceleration of an object depends on two variables, the [net force on / speed of] the object and the [direction / mass] of the object.

5. As a net force on an object increases, the acceleration of that object will [decrease / increase].

6. As the mass of an object increases (assuming the net force remains the same), the object's acceleration will [decrease / increase].

7. The unit of acceleration is [m/s^2 / kg/s].

8. The newton is a unit of [force / mass].

Newton's Second Law of Motion states that the net force on an object is equal to the mass of the object times the object's acceleration. Consider the following situation: A force of 104 N is exerted on a 52 kg object accelerating at 2 m/s^2.

For each situation below, one variable—mass, acceleration, or the net force—will change and one variable will stay constant. Predict the effect of the change on the remaining variable.

Force	Mass	Acceleration
Doubles to 108 N	Stays the same	**9.**
Stays the same	Reduced by half to 26 kg	**10.**
11.	Stays the same	Decreases to 1 m/s^2
Stays the same	Doubles to 104 kg	**12.**
Increases to 208 N	**13.**	Stays the same
Decreases to 52 N	**14.**	Stays the same

Calculating Force, Mass, and Acceleration

Newton's Second Law of Motion states a relationship between the force acting on an object, the object's mass, and its acceleration. According to Newton's second law, the acceleration of an object is equal to the net force acting on the object divided by the object's mass.

$$\text{Acceleration} = \frac{\text{Force}}{\text{Mass}} = \frac{F}{m}$$

In this equation the force (F) is measured in newtons (N), the mass (m) is usually measured in kilograms (kg). The acceleration is in m/s^2.

An object with a mass of 500 kg has a net force of 2,500 N applied to it. What is the object's acceleration?

Step 1 What do you know?

Force (F) = 2500 N

Mass (m) = 500 kg

Step 2 What are you trying to find?

Acceleration

Step 3 What formula can you use?

$$\text{Acceleration} = \frac{\text{Force}}{\text{Mass}} = \frac{F}{m}$$

Step 4 Use the numbers in the formula and solve.

$$\text{Acceleration} = \frac{\text{Force}}{\text{Mass}} = \frac{F}{m}$$

Remember that 1 N = 1kg • m/s^2; therefore change the units, and kg will cancel out.

$$a = \frac{2,500 \text{ N}}{500 \text{ kg}}$$

$$a = \frac{2,500 \text{ kg} \cdot m/s^2}{500 \text{ kg}}$$

$$a = 5 \text{ } m/s^2$$

1. An object with a mass of 65 kg comes to a stop when an 800 N force acts on the object. What is the negative acceleration on the object? _____

NAME _____   DATE _____

Newton's Third Law of Motion

Explore the nature of Newton's Third Law of Motion. For each of the statements below regarding Newton's third law, write the term or terms that will make each statement true.

1. According to Newton's third law, if you push on a wall, the wall _____.

2. According to Newton's Third Law forces always act in _____ but _____ parts.

3. When one object exerts a force on another object, the second object exerts _____ force in the _____ direction on the first object.

4. When you are walking forward you push backwards on the ground. You push the Earth backward, and the _____ pushes your shoe forward.

5. According to Newton's third law, one force is called the action force and the other force is the _____ force.

In each situation below, you are given either the action or the reaction force. Complete the force pair by identifying the missing force. Keep in mind a simple rule regarding Newton's Third law:

> **Action:** Object A exerts a force on Object B.
> **Reaction:** Object B exerts a force on Object A.

Action	Reaction
A car tire pushes on the road.	**6.**
A rocket pushes on the gas produced from the fuel.	**7.**
8.	The rope attached to the wall pulls you.
A baseball bat makes contact with a ball, exerting force on the ball.	**9.**
10.	The nail exerts an upward force on the hammer.

Friction

Explore the nature of different types of friction. For each statement below, write *ST* in the blank if the statement refers to static friction, *SL* if the statement refers to sliding friction, *R* if the statement refers to rolling friction, or *All* if the statement refers to all types of friction.

1. _____ The friction force that acts on rolling objects.

2. _____ The friction force that opposes motion of an object through a liquid or gas.

3. _____ Acts at the surface where objects are in contact, moving through a liquid, or moving through a gas.

4. _____ A force that opposes the direction of motion of an object as it moves over a surface.

5. _____ The friction force that acts on objects that are not moving.

6. _____ Ball bearings take advantage of this type of friction, greatly reducing the force needed to move an object.

Scientists "measure" friction with a number called the *coefficient of friction*. This number is the force needed to set an object in motion or keep it in motion. Just as there are different types of friction, there are different coefficients of friction. *Static friction* is the friction force acting on an object not in motion; *sliding friction* is the friction force acting on an object in motion.

Use the data in the table below to further explore friction and investigate the nature of the coefficient of friction. Fill in the blank to answer each question.

Surface	Coefficient of Friction	
	Static	Sliding
Steel on steel (dry)	0.6	0.4
Steel on steel (greasy)	0.1	0.05
Teflon on steel	0.041	0.04
Rubber tires on pavement	0.9	0.8
Metal on ice	0.022	0.02

7. Compare the coefficient of sliding friction and static friction for each set of objects (for example, steel on steel [dry]). Which is the lower value? _____

8. Based on your answer to item 7, which requires a greater input force—to set an object in motion by overcoming static friction or to keep an object moving? _____

(Gravity

Explore the nature of gravity. Classify each statement as true or false. If the statement is true, place a _T_ in the blank. Place an _F_ in the blank if the statement is false. If the statement is false, replace the underlined term with one that makes the statement true.

1. _____ Of the four universal forces (electromagnetic, strong nuclear, weak nuclear, gravity), gravity is the <u>strongest</u>. _____

2. _____ Newton discovered that gravity affects <u>all</u> objects in the universe. _____

3. _____ Gravity (or the gravitational force of attraction) between two objects depends on mass and <u>distance</u>. _____

4. _____ The greater the mass of the two objects, the <u>weaker</u> the gravitational force. _____

5. _____ The <u>greater</u> the distance between two objects, the weaker the gravitational force.

_____

6. _____ Gravity is <u>a repulsive</u> force, meaning it acts to pull objects together. _____

7. _____ Earth's gravity acts <u>upward away from</u> the Earth's center. _____

8. _____ The force of gravity (g) is a type of <u>acceleration</u>. _____

9. _____ The units for measuring the force of gravity is <u>m/s^2</u>. _____

The weight of an object is obtained by multiplying the mass of the object by the force of gravity. The force of gravity depends on the mass and radius of a planet. Larger, heavier planets have a greater force of gravity.

Suppose a 50 Kg astronaut travels to the planets in the solar system. Use the data below to determine the astronaut's weight on each planet.

Planet	Force of gravity (m/s^2)	Mass (kg)	Weight (N)
Mercury	3.61	50	**10.**
Venus	8.83	50	**11.**
Earth	9.80	50	**12.**
Mars	3.75	50	**13.**
Jupiter	26.0	50	**14.**
Saturn	11.2	50	**15.**
Uranus	10.5	50	**16.**
Neptune	13.3	50	**17.**
Pluto	0.61	50	**18.**

Momentum

Explore the nature of momentum. Classify each statement below as true or false. Place a *T* in the blank if the statement is true. Place an *F* in the blank if the statement is false. If the statement is false, replace the underlined term with a term that makes the statement true.

1. _____ The momentum of an object is the product of its mass and its <u>acceleration</u>.

   _____

2. _____ Momentum is described by its <u>direction</u> and amount (or quantity). _____

3. _____ The unit of momentum is <u>kilogram • meter/second, or kg • m/s^2</u>.

   _____

4. _____ The direction of momentum of an object is the <u>opposite</u> direction to its velocity.

   _____

5. _____ The more momentum an object has, the <u>easier</u> it is to stop. _____

6. _____ Two objects have the same velocity. The object with the greater mass will have the

   <u>greater</u> momentum. _____

7. _____ Two objects have the same mass. The object with the lower velocity will have the

   <u>greater</u> momentum. _____

Momentum is the product of an object's mass and its velocity (momentum = mass × velocity). Mass is measured in kilograms (kg), velocity in meters/second (m/s), and momentum is kilograms • meters/second (kg • m/s).

Step 1 What do you know?

Mass: 0.015 kg
Velocity: 17 m/s

Step 2 What are you trying to find?

Momentum

Step 3 What formula can you use?

Momentum = mass × velocity

Step 4 Use the numbers in the formula and solve.

Momentum = mass × velocity
= 0.015 kg × 17 m/s
= 0.26 kg • m/s

8. Which object has the greater momentum: a 4 kg object moving at 1.2 m/s or a 5 kg object

   moving at 0.75 m/s? _____

Conservation of Momentum

The law of conservation of momentum states that the total momentum of objects before they collide equals the total momentum of the objects after the collision. The collision the two objects undergo can be classified as an *elastic* or *inelastic* collision. Explore the nature of these collisions by completing the table below.

1. Elastic collisions—objects do not _____ together.		
Before Collision	**Collision**	**After Collision**
2. One object moves, one is _____.		**3.** The moving object _____; the object at rest _____.
4. Both objects are _____.		**5.** Objects _____, move in the direction _____ their original motion.
6. Objects moving in _____ direction with one moving faster.		**7.** The two objects separate. The faster object moves _____; the slower object moves _____.
8. Inelastic collisions—two objects _____ together.		
Before Collision	**Collision**	**After Collision**
9. One object _____; the other may or may not be _____.		**10.** Objects stick together, but at a velocity _____ than the beginning velocity.

A 5 kg object moves at 1m/s towards a 3 kg object at rest (velocity = 0 m/s.) The two objects collide and stick together. What is the velocity of the two objects as they move together?

Step 1 What do you know? Object 1 mass: 5 kg Object 1 velocity: 1 m/s
Object 2 mass: 3 kg Object 2 velocity: 0 m/s

Step 2 What are you trying to find? The velocity of the two objects together.

Step 3 What formula can you use? $(m_1 v_1 + m_2 v_2) = (m_1 + m_2)(v_2)$

Step 4 Use the numbers in the formula and solve. $(5 \text{ kg} \times 1 \text{ m/s}) + (3 \text{ kg} \times 0 \text{ m/s}) = (5 \text{ kg} + 3 \text{ kg})(v_2)$
$5 \text{ kg} \cdot \text{m/s} + 0 \text{ kg} \cdot \text{m/s} = (8 \text{ kg})(v_2)$

Divide each side by 8 kg $5 \text{ kg} \cdot \text{m/s} = 8 \text{ kg} (v_2)$
$\frac{5}{8} \text{ m/s} = v_2$

11. A 2 kg object moving at 4 m/s towards a 4 kg object at rest. The two objects collide and stick together. What is the speed of the objects after the collision? _____

Physical Science • © Saddleback Educational Publishing • www.sdlback.com

(*Calculating Work*

Work is defined as the product of the force exerted on an object and the distance that the object moves as the force is applied. For a force to do work on the object, the force must be in the same direction as the object moves. If the object does not move, no work is done.

Explore the nature of work by circling the term in each pair of terms that will make the statement true.

1. When calculating work, the force exerted on the object must be in [kilograms / newtons].

2. A person holding a book while walking [does / does not] do work on the book.

3. The unit used to measure work is the product of force times distance or newton-meter. The unit newton-meter is also known as a [joule / watt].

4. A person lifting a book off of a table [does / does not] do work on the book.

5. A force that does not act in the direction [does / does not] do work on the object.

As you have seen, the amount of work done is based on the force exerted on an object in the direction of motion times the distance the object moves.

A 35 N force is exerted on an object. The object moves 1.75 m in the direction of the force. What is the work done on the object?

Step 1 What do you know?   Force (F) = 35 N

                                     Distance (d) = 1.75 m

Step 2 What are you trying to find?   Work (W)

Step 3 What formula can you use? $W = F \times d$

Step 4 Use the numbers in the formula $W = F \times d$
           and solve.

                                     $W = 35 \text{ N} \times 1.75 \text{ m}$

                                     $W = 61.25 \text{ N} \bullet \text{m or } 61.25 \text{ J}$

6. An object moves 2.25 m in the direction of a force exerted on an object. The force

   exerted on the object is 75 N. What is the work done on the object? _____

(Mechanical Advantage

Explore the nature of mechanical advantage by identifying each statement as true or false. Place a *T* in the space if the statement is true and an *F* in the space if the statement is false. For each false statement, replace the underlined term with a term that will make the statement true.

1. _____ The mechanical advantage of a machine is the number of times that the

machine <u>increases</u> an output force. _____

2. _____ The mechanical advantage of a machine equals the ratio of output to the

<u>work done</u>. _____

3. _____ The <u>actual</u> mechanical advantage of a machine is the mechanical advantage

of the machine when there is no friction. _____

4. _____ The actual mechanical advantage of a machine is always <u>less</u> than the ideal

mechanical advantage of the machine. _____

5. _____ When calculating ideal mechanical advantage the input distance and output

distance is measured in <u>grams</u>. _____

If you know the input distance of a machine and the output distance of the machine, you can calculate the ideal mechanical advantage (IMA).

A ramp is used for an entrance to a building. The ramp is 2.75 m long and rises 0.75 m. What is the ideal mechanical advantage of the ramp?

Step 1 What do you know?   Ramp length (input) = 2.75m
For a ramp, the length of the ramp is the   Ramp rise (output) = 0.75 m
input; the height of the ramp is the output.

Step 2 What are you trying to find?   Ideal mechanical advantage (IMA)

Step 3 What formula can you use? $IMA = \dfrac{\text{input distance}}{\text{output distance}}$

Step 4 Use the numbers in the formula and solve. $IMA = \dfrac{\text{input distance}}{\text{output distance}}$

$IMA = \dfrac{2.75 \text{ m}}{0.75 \text{ m}}$

$IMA = 3.67$

6. A construction worker uses a lever to move a rock. The lever is moved 3 m while the rock moves 0.75 m. What is the ideal mechanical advantage of the lever? _____

Physical Science • © Saddleback Educational Publishing • www.sdlback.com

Simple Machines

Match the type of simple machine with its description. Place the letter of the description in the blank next to its matching simple machine.

1. _____ Lever
2. _____ Wedge
3. _____ Inclined plane
4. _____ Screw
5. _____ Wheel and axle
6. _____ Pulley

a. a simple machine made of two circular or cylindrical objects

b. a bar that is free to pivot about a fixed point

c. an inclined plane wrapped around a cylinder

d. a device that is thick at one end and forms a thin edge at the other end

e. a grooved wheel and a rope wrapped around the wheel

f. a flat slanted surface

The mechanical advantage of an inclined plane is determined by the following formula:

$$IMA = \frac{\text{length of the incline}}{\text{height of the incline}}$$

Compare the mechanical advantage of an inclined plane by comparing different heights of various planes.

Mass of Object	Length of Incline	Height of Incline	Input Force (Output Force)	Mechanical Advantage
30 N	5.0 m	0.35 m	15 N	**7.**
30 N	5.0 m	0.65 m	20 N	**8.**
30 N	5.0 m	0.95 m	21 N	**9.**
30 N	5.0 m	1.35 m	25 N	**10.**

11. For which combination of length and height is the mechanical advantage the greatest?

_____

12. For which combination of length and height is the input force (the force to move the object) the least? _____

13. For which combination of length and height is the mechanical advantage the least?

_____

14. What happens to the mechanical advantage as the ramp gets steeper (the height increases)? _____

Types of Levers

Compare the three types of levels by completing the table below.

Lever	Location of Input Force	Location of Output Force	Location of Fulcrum	Direction of Input and Output Force
First class	One end of the lever	1. _____ end of the lever	2. _____ the input and output force	3. In _____ direction
Second class	One end of the lever	4. _____ the fulcrum and input force	5. End opposite the _____ _____	6. In _____ direction
Third class	7. _____ the fulcrum and output force	One end of the lever	8. End opposite the _____	9. In _____ direction

For each of the levers below, complete each diagram by supplying the missing part.

First class lever	output force input force 10. _____ fulcrum
Second class lever	output force 12. _____ 11. _____ fulcrum
Third class lever	13. _____ output force 14. _____ 15. _____

Physical Science • © Saddleback Educational Publishing • www.sdlback.com

Fixed and Movable Pulleys

Explore the nature of different pulleys. Write *F* in the blank if the statement refers to a fixed pulley. Write *M* in the blank if the statement refers to a movable pulley. Write *S* in the blank if the statement refers to a pulley system. Write *A* in the blank if the statement refers to all pulleys.

1. _____ The pulley is attached to the object being moved.

2. _____ A type of simple machine.

3. _____ A combination of fixed and movable pulleys.

4. _____ The mechanical advantage of this type of pulley depends on how the pulleys are arranged.

5. _____ The pulley is attached so the pulley does not move.

6. _____ Changes only the direction of the input force.

7. _____ Changes the direction and size of the input force.

8. _____ Input force and output force are the same.

The mechanical advantage of a pulley is determined by the following formula.

$$\text{Mechanical Advantage} = \frac{\text{output force}}{\text{input force}}$$

Compare the mechanical advantage of different types of pulleys by completing the table below. Then use the data in the table to complete the statements that follow.

Type	Input Force	Output Force	Mechanical Advantage
Fixed	20 N	10 N	**9.**
	10 N	10 N	**10.**
Movable	20 N	40 N	**11.**
	5 N	10 N	**12.**
Pulley system	20 N	60 N	**13.**
	30 N	60 N	**14.**

15. The mechanical advantage of a movable pulley is _____.

16. The type of pulley with the greatest mechanical advantage is a _____.

17. You wish to lift a 30 N object using a movable pulley. To do so would require an input

force of _____.

(Pascal's Principle

Explore the nature of Pascal's principle. For each statement below, circle the term in each pair of terms that makes the statement true.

1. Pascal's principle states that when a force is applied to an enclosed liquid, an increase in pressure is transmitted [equally / unequally] to all parts of the fluid.

2. The pressure in a fluid-filled pipe is increased by 10 units of pressure. The pressure everywhere in the pipe [increases / decreases] by [10 / 20] units of pressure.

3. One application of Pascal's principle is a device that uses pressurized fluid acting on pistons of different sizes to increase force. This device is known as a [force / hydraulic] system.

4. A hydraulic system [multiplies / reduces] force by applying the force to a small surface area.

A hydraulic lift works on the principle that the pressure into the system equals the pressure out of the system. You can calculate the operation of a hydraulic system with the following equation:

$$\frac{F_{in}}{A_{in}} = \frac{F_{out}}{A_{out}}$$

The diagram below shows an auto repair station's car lift. The car on the lift weighs 12,000 N and sits on a piston with an area of 0.90 m². The other piston in the system has an area of 0.20 m².

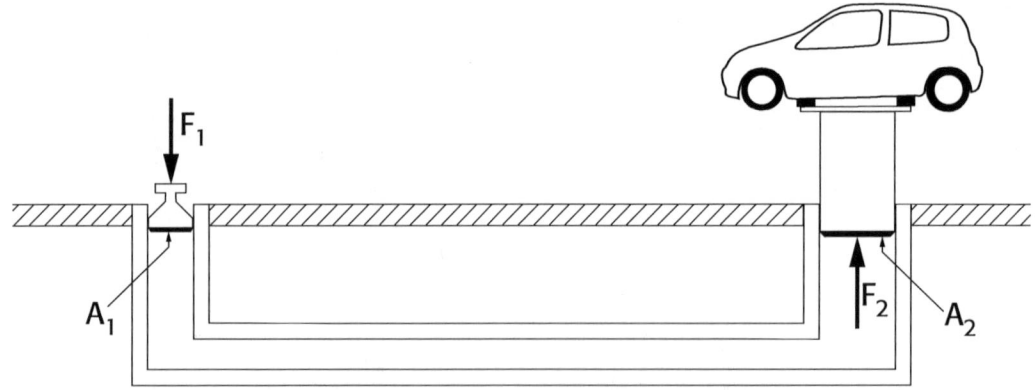

For each statement fill in each blank to make the statement true.

5. The output is the _____ of the car.

6. The output area is the area of the _____ piston.

7. The input area is the area of the _____ piston.

8. If you place the known numbers into the formula, the force needed to lift the car

   is _____ N.

Physical Science • © Saddleback Educational Publishing • www.sdlback.com

Bernoulli's Principle

Explore the nature of Bernoulli's principle. Use the diagram below to answer the following statements. For each statement, circle the term that makes each statement true.

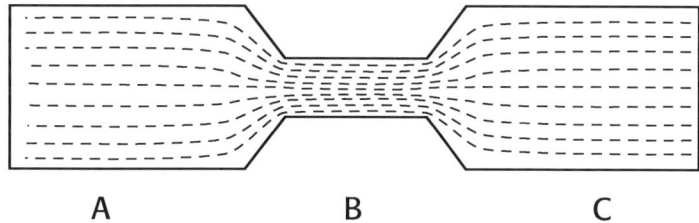

A   B   C

1. Bernoulli's principle states that when the speed of a fluid increases, the pressure of the fluid [decreases / increases].

2. According to Bernoulli's principle, in a flowing liquid pressure and speed are [directly / inversely] related.

3. In the diagram above, the amount of fluid flowing through Section A is [less than / the same as] the amount of fluid flowing through Section B.

4. In the diagram above, the amount of fluid flowing through Section C is [less than / the same as] the amount of fluid flowing through Section B.

5. The pressure in Section A is [greater than / less than] the pressure in Section B.

6. The pressure in Section B is [greater than / less than] the pressure in Section C.

7. List the sections in the diagram in order from the area of higher pressure to the area

   of lower pressure. _____

8. In the diagram above, the speed of the fluid flowing through Section A is [greater than / less than] the speed of the fluid in Section B.

9. In the diagram above, the speed of the fluid flowing through Section B is [greater than / less than] the speed of the fluid in Section C.

10. List the sections in the diagram in order from the area where the speed of the fluid is

    greatest to the area where the speed of the fluid is least. _____

11. In general, the wider the pipe or tube through which a fluid flows the [higher / lower] the pressure and the [faster / slower] the speed of the fluid.

Kinetic and Potential Energy

Compare the nature of kinetic and potential energy. For each statement below, place a *K* in the blank if the statement refers to kinetic energy, a *P* if the statement refers to potential energy, or a *B* if the statement refers to both kinetic and potential energy.

1. _____ Form of energy that depends on the mass of the object.

2. _____ The energy associated with an object in motion.

3. _____ Energy associated with an object due to its position.

4. _____ Energy that depends on the height of an object.

5. _____ Form of energy that is measured in joules (J).

6. _____ A bowling ball moving down a lane towards the pins.

7. _____ Turning the key of a wind-up toy.

8. _____ The energy of a falling object when it is halfway to the ground.

Imagine a ball on a table that is 1 meter in height. The ball is dropped from the table. The table below shows what happens to the ball as it falls. Use the data in the table to complete each of the following statements.

Time (s)	Height (m)	Speed (m/s)	PE (J)	KE (J)	Total Energy
0.0	1.0	0.00	0.74	0.00	**9.**
0.1	0.95	0.98	0.70	0.04	**10.**
0.2	0.80	2.0	0.59	0.15	**11.**
0.3	0.56	2.9	0.41	0.33	**12.**
0.4	0.22	3.9	0.16	0.58	**13.**

14. The potential energy is the greatest when the ball is _____ on the table.

15. The kinetic energy is 0 J when the ball _____ moving.

16. As the ball falls, the potential energy of the object _____.

17. As the ball falls, the speed of the object _____. As a result, the kinetic

energy _____.

18. At each time, add the PE and KE and enter the sum in the last column (total energy).

The data in the last column shows that as the ball falls the total energy _____

_____. This is because of the law of _____ of energy.

Physical Science • © Saddleback Educational Publishing • www.sdlback.com

C Calculating Kinetic Energy

Explore the nature of kinetic energy. For each statement below, circle the term that makes each statement true.

1. Kinetic energy is the energy of objects [in motion / at rest].

2. The kinetic energy of an object depends on its [mass / weight] and its [acceleration / velocity].

3. The formula for calculating the kinetic energy of an object is KE $= \frac{1}{2}mv^2$. So if you double the mass of an object (but do not change the speed), you will [cut in half / double] the object's kinetic energy.

4. Based on the formula for kinetic energy, if you double the speed of an object (without changing it's mass) the object's kinetic energy will [double / quadruple].

5. In the formula for kinetic energy, m stands for [mass / weight] and is measured in [kg / N].

6. In the formula for kinetic energy, v stands for [velocity / vector] and is measured in [m/s / m/s^2].

7. Kinetic energy is measured in [joules / kilograms].

A 10 kg object is moving at a constant speed of 6 m/s. What is the object's kinetic energy?

Step 1 What do you know?   Mass (m): 10 kg

                                                 Speed (n): 6 m/s

Step 2 What are you trying to find?   Kinetic energy

Step 3 What formula can you use?   KE $= \frac{1}{2}mv^2$

Step 4 Use the numbers in the formula   KE $= \frac{1}{2}mv^2$
           and solve.
                                                 KE $= \frac{1}{2}(10 \text{ kg})(6 \text{ m/s})^2$

                                                 KE $= \frac{1}{2}(10 \text{ kg})(36 \text{ m}^2/\text{s}^2)$

                                                 KE $= 180$ J

8. A 1200 kg car is moving down a road at 20 m/s. What is the kinetic energy of the car?

   _____

C Calculating Gravitational Potential Energy

Explore the nature of gravitational potential energy. Classify each statement as true or false. Place a *T* in the blank if the statement is true. Place an *F* in the blank if the statement is false. If the statement is false, replace the underlined term with a term that will make the statement true.

1. _____ Potential energy is the energy of an object's <u>motion</u>. _____

2. _____ One form of potential energy is <u>gravitational potential energy</u>, the energy that

depends on an object's height. _____

3. _____ The higher an object is the <u>more</u> gravitational potential energy it will have.

_____

4. _____ An object's gravitational potential energy depends on an object's <u>weight</u>, height,

and acceleration due to gravity. _____

5. _____ The formula for gravitational potential energy is PE = *mgh*. In this formula,

m stands for mass and is measured in <u>newtons</u>. _____

6. _____ In the formula for gravitational potential energy, *h* stands for the object's height

and is measured in <u>kilograms</u>. _____

7. _____ Potential energy is measured in <u>joules</u>. _____

Gravitational potential energy is the energy of an object's position (height). This type of energy is calculated by using the formula: PE = *mgh*.

A 75-kilogram construction worker stands on a platform 1.5 meters high. What is the worker's gravitational potential energy?

Step 1 What do you know?	Mass (*m*): 75 kg	
	Height (*h*): 15 m	
Step 2 What are you trying to find?	Gravitational potential energy	
Step 3 What formula can you use?	PE = *mgh*	
Step 4 Use the numbers in the formula and solve.	PE = *mgh*	
Remember *g* is gravity, which is 9.8 m/s² on Earth.	PE = (75 kg)(9.8 m/s²)(15m)	
	PE = 11,025 J	

8. A 55 kg person stands at the top of a 15 m cliff. What is the person's gravitational energy?

_____

Forms of Energy

Energy comes in many different forms. Match the type of energy with its description. Place the letter of each description in the blank next to its form of energy.

1. _____ Mechanical

2. _____ Thermal

3. _____ Chemical

4. _____ Electrical

5. _____ Electromagnetic

6. _____ Nuclear

a. the energy derived from many electric charges

b. energy stored in the chemical bonds that hold atoms together

c. the energy stored in the nucleus of an atom

d. the energy associated with the motion and position of an object

e. the total potential and kinetic energy stored in all of the particles in an object

f. a form of energy that can travel through space in the form of waves

Classify the type of energy described in each situation. Write *C* in the blank if the statement refers to chemical energy, *El* for electrical energy, *Em* for electromagnetic energy, *M* for mechanical energy, *N* for nuclear energy, and *T* for thermal energy.

7. _____ A bolt of lightning

8. _____ A moving car

9. _____ The energy stored in gasoline

10. _____ Visible light

11. _____ The energy that powers the Sun

12. _____ A moving bicycle

Energy can be converted from one form to another. For each energy conversion, supply the missing information.

Description	Starting Form of Energy	Converted to This Form of Energy
Burning of wood	Chemical	**13.**
Turning on a battery-powered CD player	**14.**	Electrical
The reaction that powers the Sun to provide light	**15.**	Electromagnetic and thermal
Burning of gasoline in an engine	**16.**	Mechanical

(*Calculating Power*

Explore the nature of power. For each statement below, fill in the blanks with the term or phrase that makes the statement true.

1. Power is the _____ of doing work.

2. Doing work at a faster rate requires _____ power.

3. To increase power, you can _____ the amount of work done in a

given time, or you can do the given amount of work in _____ time.

4. The formula for calculating power is Power = $\frac{\text{Work}}{\text{Time}}$. In this formula, work is measured

in _____.

5. In the formula calculating power, time is measured in _____.

6. Power is measured in _____.

7. Based on the formula for power, you can double the amount of power by

_____ the work done or by cutting in _____

the amount of time it takes to do the work.

To calculate the power used to perform work, you need to know the amount of work done over a certain period of time. You can determine power using the formula:

$$\text{Power} = \frac{\text{Work}}{\text{Time}}$$

Lifting a box to a shelf at a height of 2 m requires 100 J of work. It takes 2 s to perform this work. How much power is used to move the box?

Step 1 What do you know?

Work: 100 J

Time: 2 s

Step 2 What are you trying to find?

Power

Step 3 What formula can you use?

Power = $\frac{\text{Work}}{\text{Time}}$

Step 4 Use the numbers in the formula and solve.

Power = $\frac{100 \text{ J}}{2 \text{ s}}$

Power = 50 J/s or 50 N

8. An elevator does 20,000 J of work in 25 s. How much power is used to move the elevator?

_____

Physical Science • © Saddleback Educational Publishing • www.sdlback.com

Temperature and Temperature Scales

Temperature can be measured in degrees Fahrenheit, degrees Celsius, or Kelvin. Compare the three scales by completing the table below.

	Fahrenheit (°F)	Celsius (°C)	Kelvin (K)
Water boils	212	**1.**	**2.**
Normal body temperature	**3.**	37	**4.**
Room temperature	68	**5.**	**6.**
Water freezes	**7.**	**8.**	273

Explore temperature measurement. For each statement below, fill in each blank to make the statement true.

9. The SI base unit for temperature is the _____.

10. The number of units between the freezing point of water and the boiling point

of water is the same for the _____ and the Kelvin scales.

11. A degree Celsius is almost _____ as large as a degree Fahrenheit.

12. On the Kelvin scale, 0 K is also known as _____.

To convert between Celsius and Fahrenheit scale, you use the following formulas:

To convert to the Celsius Scale: $°C = \frac{5}{9}(°F - 32)$

To convert to the Fahrenheit scale: $°F = \frac{9}{5}(°C) + 32$

Examples:

Convert 55°F to degrees Celsius.

$°C = \frac{5}{9}(°F - 32)$

$°C = \frac{5}{9}(55 - 32)$

$°C = \frac{5}{9}(23)$

$°C = 12.78$

Convert 30°C to degrees Fahrenheit.

$°F = \frac{9}{5}(°C) + 32$

$°F = \frac{9}{5}(30) + 32$

$°F = (54) + 32$

$°F = 86$

Convert the following temperatures.

13. 25°F to °C _____

14. 15°C to °F _____

15. 73°F to °C _____

16. 101°C to °F _____

Heat Transfer

Compare the ways in which heat is transferred. Write *Cd* in the blank if the statement refers to conduction, *Cv* if the statement refers to convection, and *Rd* if the statement refers to radiation.

   1. _____ The transfer of thermal energy when particles of a fluid move from place to place.

   2. _____ The transfer of energy through space without the help of matter to carry the energy.

   3. _____ The type of energy from air that carries the energy of the Sun to Earth.

   4. _____ Occurs within a material or between materials that are touching.

   5. _____ Air circulating in an oven.

   6. _____ The type of heat transfer common to all objects.

   7. _____ This type of transfer occurs as particles vibrate in place and push on each other.

   8. _____ This type of heat transfer is important in many cycles in nature, such as ocean currents, weather systems, and hot rock in the Earth's interior.

For each statement below, circle the term in each pair of terms that makes the statement true.

   9. Materials that allow the transfer of heat are known as [conductors / insulators].

   10. Metals are [good / poor] conductors of heat.

   11. Wood, air, and foam are non-metals. They are examples of materials that are [good / poor] conductors of heat.

   12. Materials that delay or prevent the transfer of heat are known as [conductors / insulators].

   13. Liquids and [solids / gases] are good insulators.

   14. Heat energy, energy that is transferred by radiation, is called [mechanical / radiant] energy.

   15. Conduction is explained by the [collision / repulsion] between atoms and molecules.

   16. Convection is a type of heat that occurs in [metals / liquids].

Physical Science • © Saddleback Educational Publishing • www.sdlback.com

(Specific Heat

Some materials absorb heat more readily than others. The table below shows the specific heats of some materials. Use this data to complete each statement below.

1. Specific heat is the amount of heat needed to raise the temperature of _____ gram of material by _____ degree(s) Celsius.

Specific Heats of Some Materials	
Material	**Specific Heat (J/g • °C)**
Water	4.18
Plastic	1.84
Air	1.01
Iron	0.449
Silver	0.235

2. The substance that will take the greatest amount of energy to raise 1 gram of that substance by 1°C is _____.

3. The substance that will take the least amount of energy to raise 1 gram of that substance by 1°C is _____.

4. Iron and silver are metals; air is a mixture of gases (which are non-metals). Based on the data, metals have a _____ specific heat.

Specific heat is the amount of heat needed to raise 1 g of material by 1°C. The amount of heat absorbed (or released) depends, in part, on the specific heat. The equation below will calculate the amount of heat absorbed or released by a material.

$$Q = m \times c \times T$$

A 50 g piece of iron starts at 20°C and its temperature is raised to 100°C. The specific heat of iron is 0.45 J/g • °C. How much heat is absorbed by the iron?

Step 1 What do you know?
To find the change in temperature (T), subtract the beginning temperature from the ending temperature.

Mass of iron (m): 50 g
Specific heat (c): 0.45J/g • °C
Beginning and ending temperature: 20°C and 100°C

Step 2 What are you trying to find?

Heat absorbed (Q)

Step 3 What formula can you use?

$Q = m \times c \times T$

Step 4 Use the numbers in the formula and solve.
Grams and °C cancel out, leaving J for the answer.

$Q = m \times c \times T$
$Q = (50 \text{ g})(0.45\text{J/g} • °C)(80°C)$
$Q = 1,800 \text{ J}$

5. A 250 g piece of silver starts at 35°C and its temperature is raised to 50°C. The specific heat of iron is 0.235 J/g • °C. How much heat is absorbed by the silver? _____

Laws of Thermodynamics

Compare the three laws of thermodynamics. For each statement below, identify the law of thermodynamics being described.

1. _____ Heat will flow from a cold object to a hot object only if work is done on the system.

2. _____ Absolute zero cannot be reached.

3. _____ Energy is conserved.

4. _____ A refrigerator must do work to transfer thermal energy from the cold food area to the warm room air.

5. _____ Heat can be made to flow from cold to hot by using an external effort.

6. _____ When heat is added to a system, it transforms to an equal amount of some other form of energy.

The first law of thermodynamics states that a change in the internal energy of a system is equal to the energy transferred in the form of heat minus the energy transferred by work, or

Changes in internal energy = heat transferred – work

U $=$ Q $-$ W

In this equation, all the quantities are measured in joules (J).

A total of 130 J of work is done on a system. During this process the internal energy of the system increases by 100 J. What is the amount of energy transferred by heat?

Step 1	What do you know?	Work (W): –130 J
	Because work is done on the system, it is a negative.	Internal energy (U): 100 J
Step 2	What are you trying to find?	Heat energy (Q)
Step 3	What formula can you use?	$U = Q - W$
Step 4	Use the numbers in the formula and solve.	$U = Q - W$
		100 J = Q – (–130 J)
		100 J = Q + 130 J
		–30 J = Q

7. A total of 45 J of heat is added to a system. At the same time, 25 J of work is done on

the system. What is the change in the system's internal energy? _____

Heat Engines

The work of a heat engine is shown in the diagram below. Complete each diagram to show the flow of energy and how and where work is done.

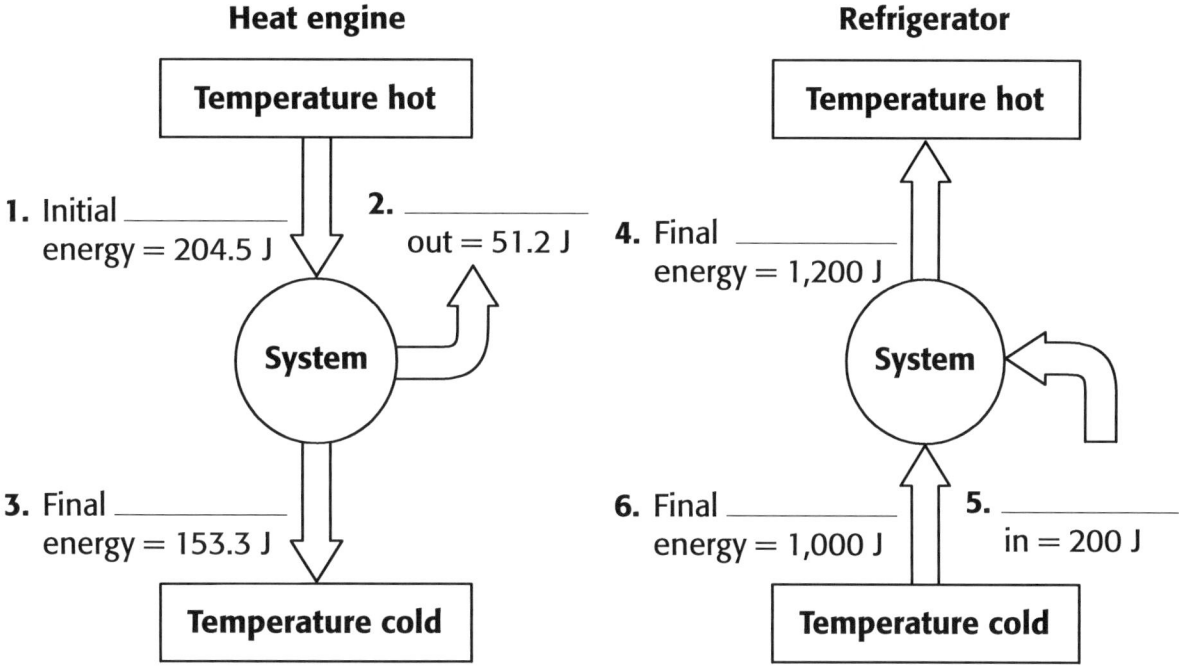

Heat engine

Temperature hot

1. Initial _____ energy = 204.5 J

2. _____ out = 51.2 J

System

3. Final _____ energy = 153.3 J

Temperature cold

Refrigerator

Temperature hot

4. Final _____ energy = 1,200 J

System

6. Final _____ energy = 1,000 J

5. _____ in = 200 J

Temperature cold

Explore the nature of a heat engine. For each statement below, fill in the blank with a term that will make each statement true.

7. In a heat engine, the heat energy flows from an area of _____

temperature to an area of _____ temperature.

8. In a heat engine, the system in the cylinder, the heat energy out of the system, is the

_____ from the engine.

9. In the heat engine, the heat energy into the system is 204.5 J. The energy out of the

system is the heat energy out of the system, _____, plus the mechanical energy

(work) out of the system, _____ or a total of _____.

10. In a refrigerator, work is done to move the heat energy from the _____

area to a _____ area.

11. In a refrigerator, the energy into the system is the heat energy removed from the cold

area, _____, plus the mechanical energy needed to move the heat energy to

the hot area, _____, or a total of _____.

Properties of Waves

Explore the properties of a mechanical wave. Label each part of the wave shown below.

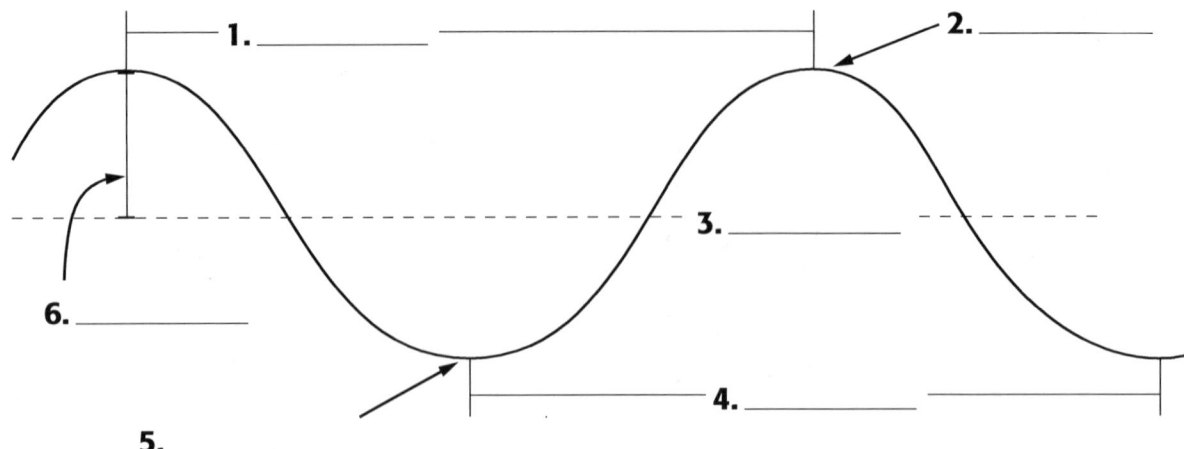

1. _____
2. _____
3. _____
4. _____
5. _____
6. _____

Match each of the properties of a mechanical wave with its description. Place the letter of the matching description in the blank next to the property term.

7. _____ Frequency

8. _____ Period

9. _____ Crest

10. _____ Trough

11. _____ Wavelength

12. _____ Amplitude

13. _____ Speed

a. equals the wavelength times the frequency

b. the number of cycles per unit of time or the number of crests (or troughs) passing a given point per unit of time

c. the highest point of a wave above the rest position

d. the distance between two adjacent crests (or two adjacent troughs)

e. the time it takes for one complete wave cycle

g. the maximum displacement of wave or the height of the crest above the rest position

For each statement below, circle the term in each pair of terms that makes the statement true.

14. In a wave, two crests pass a given point each second. The wave has a frequency of [$\frac{1}{2}$ hertz / 2 hertz].

15. Increasing the frequency of a wave [decreases / increases] its wavelength.

16. You can calculate the speed of a wave by multiplying the wave speed by its [frequency / wavelength].

17. The more energy a wave has, the [greater / lower] its amplitude.

Physical Science • © Saddleback Educational Publishing • www.sdlback.com

Types of Waves

Compare the types of mechanical waves. Place an *L* in the blank if the statement refers to a longitudinal wave, a *T* if the statement refers to a transverse wave, or an *S* if the statement refers to a surface wave. Write *All* in the blank if the statement refers to all types of mechanical waves.

1. _____ A wave that vibrates at right angles to the direction in which the wave moves.

2. _____ Matter is required for the wave to travel through.

3. _____ A wave created by shaking a rope up and down.

4. _____ A wave in which the vibrations are parallel to the direction that the wave travels.

5. _____ A wave that travels along a surface separating two media.

6. _____ A wave that travels as a result of compressions and refractions.

7. _____ A disturbance in matter that carries energy from one place to another.

Explore the nature of transverse and longitudinal waves. The diagram below shows a transverse wave and a longitudinal wave. Identify each type of wave and label the parts of each wave.

Transverse Wave

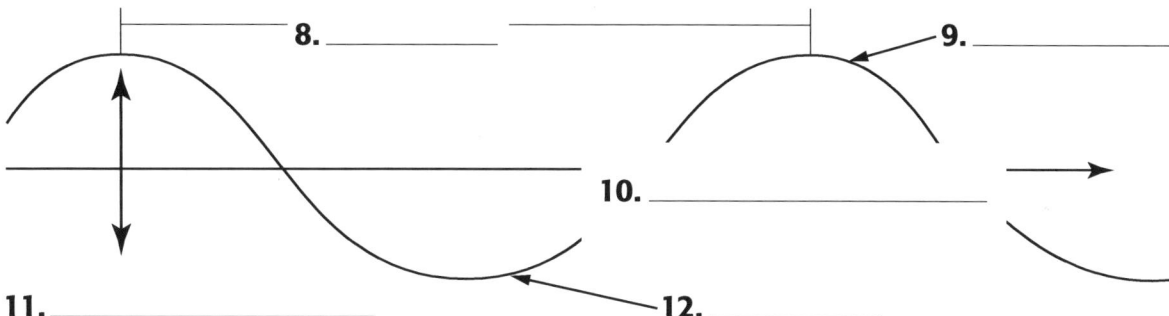

Longitudinal Wave

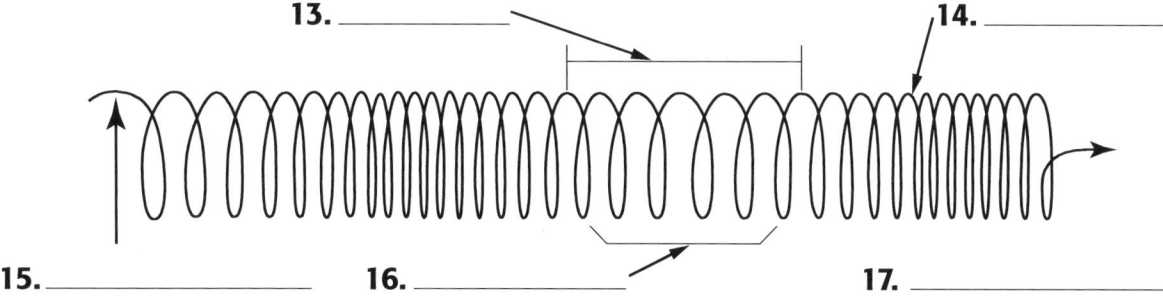

C *Calculating Wave Speed*

The speed of a wave, like the speed of a car, is how far the wave travels in a certain period of time. Explore the nature of wave speed. Classify each statement as true or false. Place a *T* in the blank if the statement is true. Place an *F* in the blank if the statement is false. For each false statement, replace the underlined term with a term that makes the statement correct.

1. _____ The formula for wave speed is Wave speed = wavelength × frequency.

   Wavelength could be measured in <u>grams</u>. _____

2. _____ In the formula for wave speed, the frequency is measured in <u>meters per

   second (m/s)</u>. _____

3. _____ The unit for wave speed can be <u>meters per second (m/s)</u>. _____

4. _____ According to the formula for wave speed, if the wavelength increases and the

   frequency remains the same, then the wave's speed <u>decreases</u>. _____

5. _____ According to the formula for wave speed, if the wavelength remains the same and

   the frequency increases, then the speed of the wave <u>increases</u>. _____

6. _____ To decrease the speed of a wave, you can <u>decrease</u> the wavelength or the

   frequency. _____

The speed of a wave is how far it travels in a certain amount of time. Another way to look at wave speed is using the formula: Wave speed = wave length × frequency, where wavelength can be in meters (m) and frequency in hertz (Hz). The resulting wave speed is in meters/second (m/s).

A wave with a wavelength of 0.50 m has a frequency of 4 Hz. What is the speed of the wave?

Step 1	What do you know?	Wavelength: 0.05 m Frequency: 4 Hz
Step 2	What are you trying to find?	Wave speed
Step 3	What formula can you use?	Wave speed = wave length × frequency
Step 4	Use the numbers in the formula and solve.	Wave speed = 0.50 m × 4 Hz
		Wave speed = 2.0 m/s
	A hertz is cycled per second, so change the 4 Hz to 4/s	

7. A wave has a length of 1.5 m and a frequency of 0.25 hertz. What is the speed of the

   wave? _____

(*Wave Interference*

Explore the nature of wave interference. For each statement, circle the term in each pair of terms that makes the statement true.

1. This displacement of waves [add together / subtract from each other] in constructive interference.

2. In [constructive / destructive] wave interference, two or more waves combine and their displacements are subtracted from each other.

3. [Constructive / Destructive] wave interference occurs when two or more waves combine and their displacements are added together.

4. Two crests (or two troughs) of a wave meet at the same point. The result is a wave with [increased / decreased] amplitude. This is an example of [constructive / destructive] interference.

Explore the nature of constructive wave interference. The graphs below show two waves that interact with each other. Examine the graphs and then fill in each blank to complete the statements that follow.

5. In Wave 1 point A is a _____

and in Wave 2 point A is a _____ .

6. In Wave 1 point B is a _____

and in Wave 2 point B is a _____ .

7. In Wave 1 point C is a _____

and in Wave 2 point C is a _____ .

8. In this example, the wave crests and troughs

occur at the _____ point.

Therefore, the amplitude is _____ .

9. The resulting amplitude at point A is

_____ units, at point B, _____

units, and at point C, _____ units.

Plot these points on a blank graph and draw

a smooth curve connecting the points.

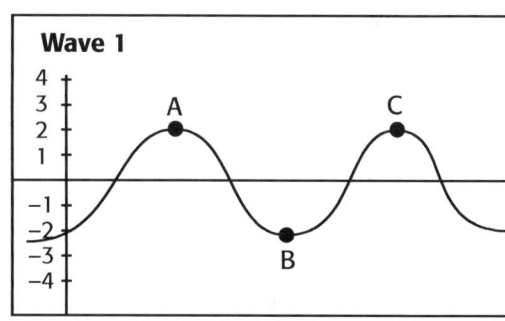

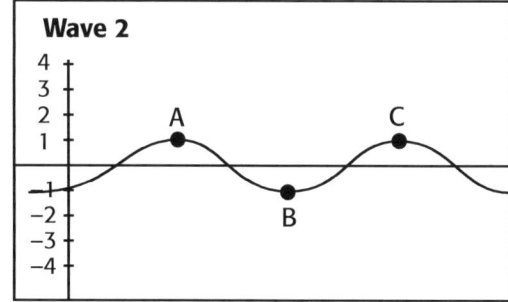

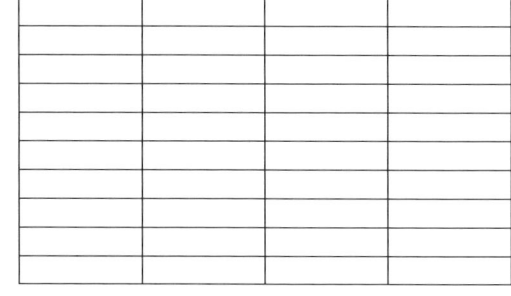

Wave Reflection and Refraction

Explore the nature of reflected light. Complete the diagram below of light reflecting off of a surface. Then, for each statement circle the term in each pair that makes the statement true.

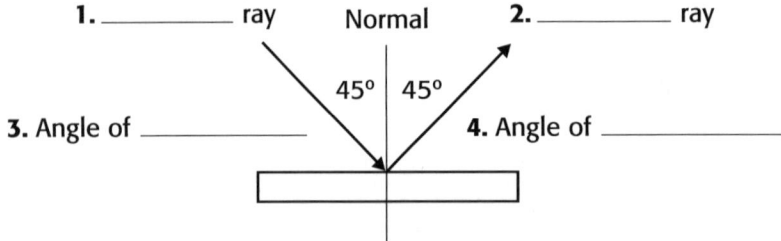

1. _____ ray   Normal   2. _____ ray

45° 45°

3. Angle of _____   4. Angle of _____

5. The ray of light approaching the surface is known as the [incident / reflected] ray.

6. The ray of light that leaves the surface is known as the [incident / reflected] ray.

7. The angle formed between the incoming ray and the normal is the angle of [incidence / reflection].

8. The angle formed between the ray coming off of the surface and the normal is the angle of [incidence / reflection].

9. The law of reflection states that when a ray of light reflects off of a surface, the angle of the incoming ray [equals / is greater than] the angle of the outgoing reflected ray.

The diagram below shows the behavior of light as it passes from one material to another. For each statement fill in the term that makes the statement true.

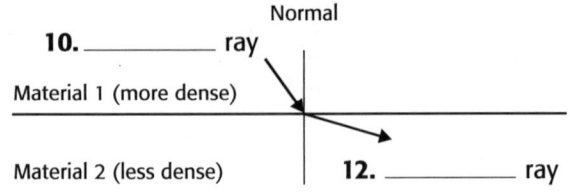

Normal

10. _____ ray

Material 1 (more dense)

Material 2 (less dense)   12. _____ ray

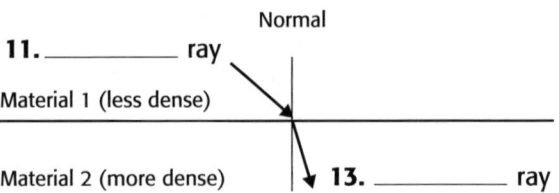

Normal

11. _____ ray

Material 1 (less dense)

Material 2 (more dense)   13. _____ ray

14. When light passes from a more dense material to a less dense material, it will bend

_____ from the normal.

15. When light passes from a less dense material to a denser material, it will bend

_____ the normal.

16. Light passing across a boundary from a less dense material to a denser material travels

_____ in the dense material.

17. Light passing across a boundary to a less dense material travels _____

in the less dense material.

    Physical Science • © Saddleback Educational Publishing • www.sdlback.com

(Properties of Sound

Explore the properties of sound. Label each statement as true or false. Place a _T_ in the blank if the statement is true. Place an _F_ in the blank if the statement is false. If the statement is false, replace the underlined term with a term that makes the statement true.

1. _____ Sound waves are <u>transverse</u> waves—waves with compressions and rarefactions that travel through a medium. _____

2. _____ In air, the speed of sound is about <u>330 m/s</u>. _____

3. _____ The speed of sound is <u>faster</u> in solids than in liquids or gases. _____

4. _____ Sound <u>pitch</u> is the rate at which energy of the wave travels through a given area. _____

5. _____ Sound intensity depends on the <u>wavelength</u> of the wave and distance from the sound source. _____

6. _____ The <u>frequency</u> depends on how fast the source of the sound is vibrating.
   _____

7. _____ Sound intensity is measured in <u>meters</u>. _____

8. _____ <u>Pitch</u> is the frequency of sound as a person hears that sound. _____

The table below shows how fast sound travels through different materials. Use the information in the table to complete each statement below.

9. Sound travels fastest in _____ and slowest in _____.

10. Compare the speed of sound in water at 0°C and at 30°C. Sound travels _____ at a higher temperature.

11. Air is a gas, water is a liquid, and aluminum is a solid. Sound waves travel _____ in solids and slowest in _____.

12. The particles in aluminum are very close together, while the particles in a gas are far apart. In general, the _____ together the particles are, the faster the wave travels.

Speed of Sound	
Material	**Speed (m/s)**
Air (0°C)	330
Air (20°C)	342
Water (0°C)	1,402
Water (30°C)	1,509
Sea water (0°C)	1,449
Sea water (30°C)	1,546
Iron	4,480
Aluminum	5,000

The Doppler Effect

The Doppler effect is observed whenever the source of a sound wave is moving with respect to an observer hearing the sound. The diagrams below show two sound sources, one moving and one not moving.

Stationary Object

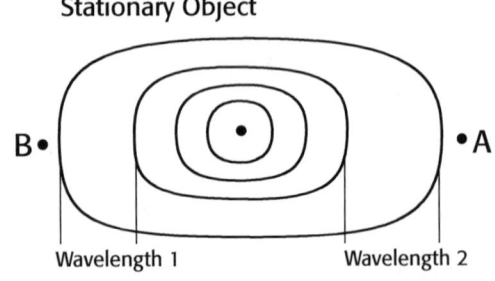

Wavelength 1   Wavelength 2

Moving Object

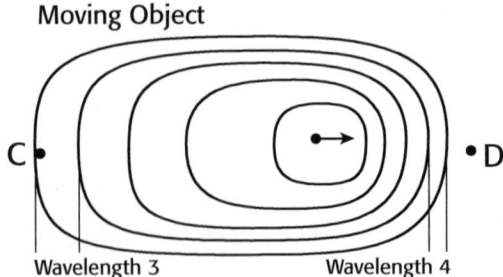

Wavelength 3   Wavelength 4

Explore the nature of the Doppler effect. Classify each of the statements below as true or false. Place a *T* in the space if the statement is true and an *F* in the space if the statement is false. For each false statement, replace the underlined term with a term that will make the statement true.

1. _____ In the Stationary Object diagram the sound source is not moving. The length of Wavelength 1 and Wavelength 2 are <u>unequal</u>. _____

2. _____ A person at Point A will receive the wave from the normal source at the same rate (frequency) as a person at Point B. Therefore, the pitch of the sound heard by each person is <u>the same</u>. _____

3. _____ In the Moving Object diagram, the sound source is moving to the right. Each sound wave produced by the source starts closer to the <u>Point C</u> and farther from <u>Point D</u>. _____

4. _____ Because the sound source is moving to the right, each sound wave has a <u>longer</u> distance to travel to reach Point D. _____

5. _____ The sound source produces a sound at constant frequency. But, because the source is moving to the right, the distance between waves at Point D is <u>shorter</u> and the frequency is <u>higher</u>. _____

6. _____ Therefore, as the sound source moves towards Point D, the wave reaches at a <u>lower</u> pitch. _____

7. _____ Because the sound source is moving to the right, each sound wave has a <u>longer</u> distance to travel to reach Point C. _____

Electromagnetic Spectrum

Explore the nature of the electromagnetic spectrum. The table below lists the types of electromagnetic waves. Complete the table by listing an everyday use of each type of wave. Then place each type in the table below.

Type	Wavelength Range	Frequency Range	Application
Gamma rays	0.1 nm to 1×10^{-5} nm	3×10^{18} Hz to 3×10^{22} Hz	**1.**
Infrared waves	0.1 nm to 700 nm	3×10^{11} Hz to 4×10^{14} Hz	**2.**
Microwaves	30 cm to 1 mm	1×10^{9} Hz to 3×10^{11} Hz	**3.**
Radio waves	Less than 30 cm	Less than 1×10^{9} Hz	**4.**
Ultraviolet light	400 nm to 60 nm	7.5×10^{14} Hz to 5×10^{15} Hz	**5.**
Visible light	700 nm to 400 nm	4×10^{14} Hz to 7×10^{14} Hz	**6.**
X-rays	60 nm to 1×10^{-4} nm	5×10^{15} Hz to 3×10^{21} Hz	**7.**

Use the data in the table to further explore the electromagnetic spectrum. Complete each statement by filling in each blank with the word(s) that make each statement true.

8. The electromagnetic waves with the longest wavelength are _____;

the electromagnetic waves with the shortest wavelength are _____.

9. The electromagnetic waves with the lowest frequency are _____;

the electromagnetic waves with the highest frequency are _____.

10. In general, the longer the wavelength the _____ the frequency;

therefore, wavelength and frequency are _____ related.

11. An electromagnetic wave has a wavelength of 350 nm. This wave belongs to the

_____ part of the electromagnetic spectrum.

Concave Mirrors

Mirrors are often made of a piece of glass that is coated with a layer of shiny metal, such as silver, on one surface.

Explore the nature of concave mirrors. For each statement below, circle the term in each pair that makes the statement true.

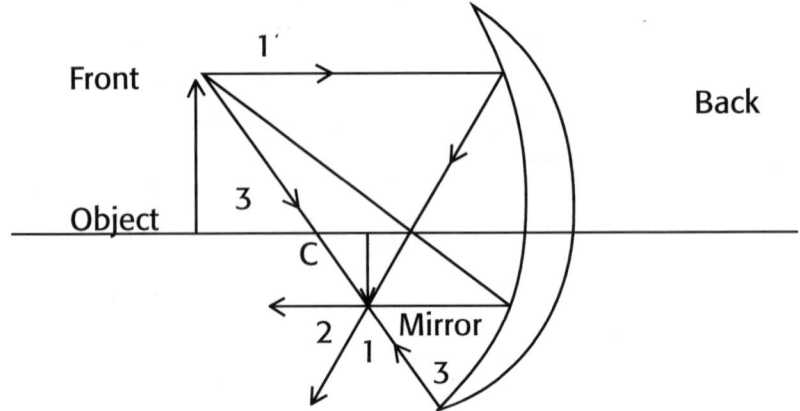

1. A concave mirror is an [inwardly / outwardly] curved mirrored surface.

2. A concave mirror [reflects / refracts] light.

3. When parallel incoming rays strike a concave mirror, they are reflected through the [curvature / focal] point.

4. Concave mirrors form a [real / virtual] image that is [upright / upside down] when reflected rays converge in front of the mirror.

Use the diagram above to complete the table outlining the rules for creating a concave mirror diagram.

Rules for Drawing a Ray Diagram		
Ray	**Line from Object to Mirror**	**Line from Mirror**
1	**5.** _____ along principal axis	**6.** Through the _____ point (F)
2	**7.** Through the _____ point (F)	Straight along principal axis
3	**8.** Through the _____ _____ (C)	Back through the center of curvature

Convex Mirrors

Mirrors are often made of a piece of glass that is coated with a layer of a shiny metal, such as silver, on one side of its surface.

Explore the nature of convex mirrors. For each statement below, circle the term in each pair of terms that makes the statement true.

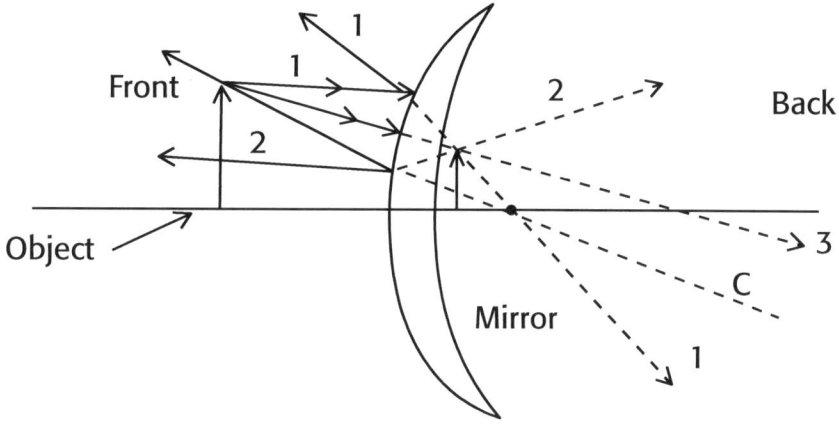

1. A convex mirror is an [inwardly / outwardly] curved mirrored surface.

2. A convex mirror [reflects / refracts] light.

3. When parallel incoming rays strike a convex mirror they appear to meet at the [curvature / focal] point.

4. In a convex mirror the focal point and center of curvature appear to be [behind / in front of] the mirror.

5. Convex mirrors form a [real / virtual] image that is [upright / up side down] when the reflected rays appear to converge behind the mirror.

Use the diagram above to complete the table outlining the rules for creating a convex mirror diagram.

Rules for Drawing a Ray Diagram		
Ray	**Line from Object to Mirror**	**Line from Mirror**
1	**6.** _____ to the mirror	**7.** Appears to go through the _____ point
2	**8.** Line towards the _____ point	**9.** Point appears to travel _____ to the principal axis behind the mirror

Concave Lenses

A lens is an optical tool that refracts (bends) light. There are two basic types of lenses, convex and concave.

Explore the nature of a concave lens. For each statement below, circle the term in each pair that makes the statement true.

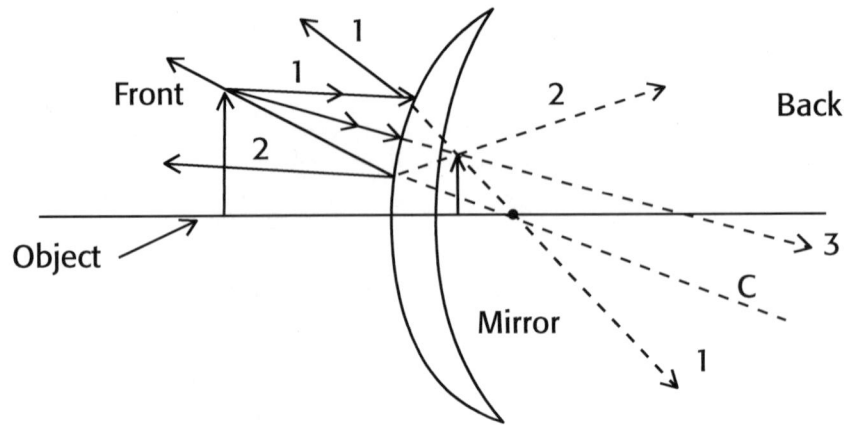

1. A concave lens is [thick / thin] in the middle and [thick / thin] at the edges.

2. A concave lens is a lens in which light [converges / diverges].

3. Light passing through a concave lens is refracted (bent) [inward / outward].

4. In a concave lens, an image usually forms on the [opposite / same] side of the lens as the object.

5. In a concave lens, the image formed is a [real / virtual] image.

6. In a concave lens, the image formed is [upright / upside down].

Use the diagram above to complete the table outlining the rules for creating a concave lens diagram.

Rules for Drawing a Ray Diagram		
Ray	**Line from Object to Lens**	**Line from Lens**
Top parallel ray	7. _____ line to lens	8. Runs a dotted line _____ from lens to focal point
Bottom (focal) ray	9. _____ line to the _____ of the lens	10. Travels in a _____ line from the lens

Physical Science • © Saddleback Educational Publishing • www.sdlback.com

(Convex Lenses

A lens is an optical tool that refracts (bends) light. There are two basic types of lenses, convex and concave.

Explore the nature of convex lenses. For each statement below, circle the term in each pair that makes the statement true.

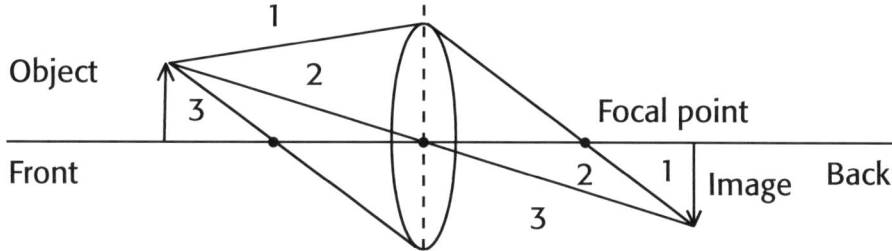

1. A convex lens is [thick / thin] in the middle and [thick / thin] at the edges.

2. A convex lens is a lens in which light [converges / diverges].

3. Light passing through a convex lens is refracted (bent) [inward / outward].

4. In a convex lens, parallel light rays passing through the lens meet at the [focal / light] point.

5. In a convex lens, an image forming in the side opposite the object is a [real / virtual] image.

6. In a convex lens, the image formed on the side opposite the object is [upright / upside down].

Use the diagram above to complete the table outlining the rules for creating a convex lens diagram.

Rules for Drawing a Ray Diagram		
Ray	**Line from Object to Lens**	**Line from Lens**
Top parallel ray	**7.** _____ line to lens	**8.** Line through the _____ point
Middle ray	**9.** To _____ of the lens	**10.** From the _____ of the lens
Bottom (focal) ray	**11.** Line through the _____ point	**12.** _____ line from the lens

(Color

The combination of absorbed and reflected light gives an object its color. Objects themselves do not have color. Color is based on the light received by the eyes and how your brain interprets the nerve impulses from the eyes to the brain.

Explore the nature of light and color. Classify each statement below as true or false. Place a *T* in the blank if the statement is true and an *F* in the blank if the statement is false. For each false statement, replace the underlined term with one that will make the statement true.

1. _____ An apple has a red color because red light is <u>absorbed</u>. _____

2. _____ All the colors of light combine to form the color <u>black</u>. _____

3. _____ An object appears to be <u>white</u> because all the colors of light have been absorbed.

_____

4. _____ An object appears to be <u>white</u> because all the colors of light have been reflected.

_____

5. _____ The <u>primary</u> colors of light are red, green, and blue. _____

6. _____ Combing two primary colors produces a <u>secondary</u> color. _____

7. _____ Red, green, and blue combined in equal amounts produce <u>black</u> light. _____

The triangle shows the primary and secondary colors of light. Red, green, and blue are the primary colors. The color in between two primary colors is a secondary color.

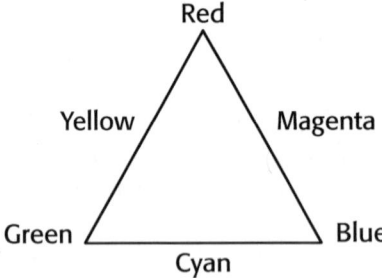

Explore the nature of color mixing. The table below shows different combinations of primary and secondary colors. For each combination, write the color that results.

Color #1	Color #2	Resulting Color
Red	Green	**8.**
Red	Blue	**9.**
Red	Cyan	**10.**
Magenta	Cyan	**11.**

Physical Science • © Saddleback Educational Publishing • www.sdlback.com

Magnets and Magnetism

A magnet is surrounded by a magnetic field. Explore the nature of magnetic fields.

1. For the single magnet below draw field lines. Then for the pair of magnets draw field lines showing how the magnetic fields interact.

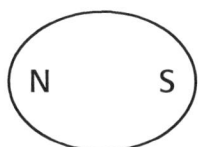

Pole Pairing	Interaction Between Poles
North – North	**2.**
North – South	**3.**
South – North	**4.**
South – South	**5.**

Explore the nature of magnets and magnetism. For each statement below, circle the term in each pair of terms that makes the statement true.

6. The parts of a magnet where magnetism is the strongest are the magnetic [domains / poles].

7. Every magnet has [four / two] poles.

8. Opposite poles of a magnet will [attract / repel].

9. Like poles of a magnet will [attract / repel].

10. If you break a bar magnet between the two poles, the result is two smaller magnets, each of which has [three / two] poles.

11. A group of atoms whose magnetic fields are aligned produce a magnetic [domain / pole].

C Electric Charges

An electric charge is surrounded by an electric field. Explore the nature of electric fields associated with electric charges and the interaction between electric fields.

1. For the positive and negative charges draw field lines for each. Then for the pairs of charges draw field lines showing how the electric fields interact.

Pole Pairing	Interaction Between Charges
Positive – Negative	**2.**
Positive – Positive	**3.**
Negative – Negative	**4.**
Negative – Positive	**5.**

Explore the nature of electric charges and electric fields. Classify each statement as true or false. Place a *T* in the blank if the statement is true. Place an *F* in the blank if the statement is false. For each false statement, replace the underlined term with a term to make the statement true.

6. _____ There are <u>two</u> types of charges. _____

7. _____ A negative charge will <u>attract</u> another negative charge. _____

8. _____ A negatively charged object has had <u>protons</u> transferred to it. _____

9. _____ If electrons are transferred from one neutral object to another neutral object, the

object losing electrons becomes <u>negatively</u> charged. _____

10. _____ Materials in which electric charges move freely are called <u>conductors</u>; materials in

which electric charges do not move freely are <u>insulators</u>. _____

11. _____ You rub a balloon against your hair. Both your hairs and the balloon become

charged. This is an example of charging by <u>contact</u>. _____

Physical Science • © Saddleback Educational Publishing • www.sdlback.com

C Ohm's Law

Ohm's Law allows you to calculate the amount of current carried through a circuit. Explore the nature of Ohm's Law. For each statement, circle the term in each pair of terms that makes the statement true.

1. The unit of electric current is the [ampere / volt].

2. The amount of current that flows through a circuit depends on the [charge / voltage] and resistance in the circuit.

3. According to Ohm's Law, the voltage in a circuit is the result of multiplying the [current / potential difference] by the resistance, or $V = IR$.

4. If you increase the voltage (V) in a circuit, the current (I) will [decrease / increase].

5. According to Ohm's Law, if you keep the voltage (V) the same and increase the resistance (R), the current (I) will [decrease / increase].

Complete the table below regarding Ohm's Law:

Ohm's Law: $V = IR$		
Variable	**Description**	**Units**
V	6.	7.
I	8.	9.
R	10.	11.

A wire carries a 7.5 A current. The resistance in the wire is 0.5 Ω. What is the voltage?

Step 1 What do you know?   Current (I): 7.5 A
                                             Resistance (R): 0.5 W

Step 2 What are you trying to find?   Voltage (V)

Step 3 What formula can you use?   voltage = current × resistance: $V = IR$

Step 4 Use the numbers in the formula and solve. $V = IR$
                                             $V = (7.5 \text{ A})(0.5 \text{ Ω})$
                                             $V = 3.75 \text{ V}$

12. What is the voltage in a wire that carries a current of 15 A and has a resistance of 1.5 Ω?

_____

Electric Circuits–Introduction

Creating a circuit diagram shows electric circuits. Match the circuit symbol with the part of the circuit it represents.

1. _____ Wire

2. _____ Resistor

3. _____ Bulb

4. _____ Power source

5. _____ Switch (open)

6. _____ Electric plug

7. _____ Switch (closed)

a. ─────◯───

b. ───○───○───

c. ─────+┤ ┠─────

d. ───────∿∿∿───────

e. ────⬭────

f. ─────────

g. ───○╱ ○───

Label each part of the circuit diagram shown below.

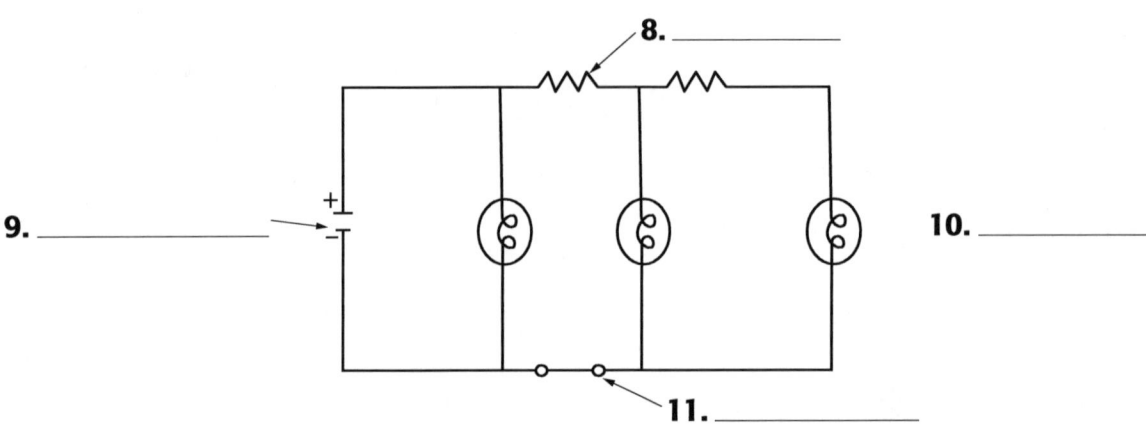

8. _____

9. _____

10. _____

11. _____

12. Draw a circuit diagram with the following parts: two power sources, two bulbs, one resistor, and an open switch.

Series Circuits

Below is a circuit diagram in which three resistors are connected in series. Several rules govern the behavior of a series circuit.

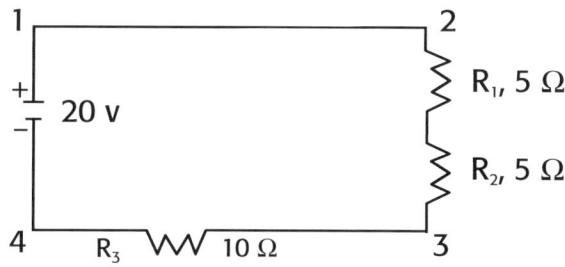

Before looking at the rules, let's look at some of the features of the circuit. Fill in the blank in each of the following statements.

1. In a series circuit all parts are _____ to each other in one long chain.

2. In this circuit the current moves from the _____ terminal to the

_____ terminal.

Rule 1:

3. The current of the circuit was measured at points 1–4 with the following results:

  Point 1: 2 A   Point 2: 2 A   Point 3: 2 A   Point 4: 2 A

Therefore, in a series circuit the _____ current moves through each part of the circuit.

Rule 2:

4. The total resistance in the circuit was measured at 20 Ω. The resistance at R_1 is _____,

at R_2 it is _____, and at R_3 it is _____.

Therefore, in a series circuit the total resistance is equal to the _____ of the individual resistances.

Rule 3:

5. Next, the voltage drop across each resistor is measured. The *voltage drop* is the amount the voltage lowers when crossing a resistor. The voltage drops across each resistor are:

  Across R1: 5V   Across R2: 5V   Across R3: 10 V

  Total drop: _____   The voltage of the battery: _____

Therefore, the voltage applied to a series circuit is equal to the _____ of the individual voltage drops.

Rule 4:

6. The circuit was broken at point 4. The current at points 3, 2, and 1 are 0 A.

Therefore, in a series circuit, if the circuit is broken at any point, _____ current will flow.

Parallel Circuits

Many electrical circuits have more than one device (such as a bulb or resistor) that receives electrical energy. These devices are usually connected in series or parallel.

Below is a circuit diagram in which two resistors are connected in parallel. Several rules govern the behavior of a parallel circuit.

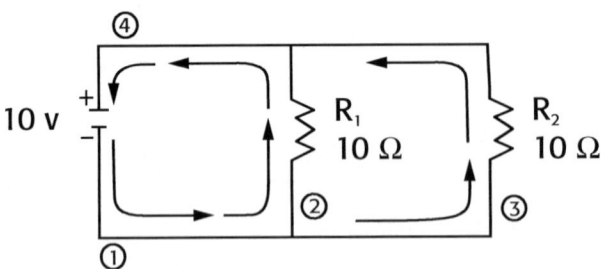

Fill in the blank in each statement to make the statement true.

Rule 1:

1. The arrows in the circuit diagram show the movement of the _____.

   In a parallel circuit, there is _____ one path for the current to move.

Rule 2:

2. The voltage in the circuit was measured across each resistor with the following results:

   Across R_1: 10 V   Across R_2: 10 V

   Therefore, in a parallel circuit, the voltage is _____ across each part of the circuit.

Rule 3:

3. At points 1–4 the current was measured with the following results:

   Point 1: 2 A   Point 3: 1 A   Point 2: 1 A   Point 4: 2 A

   The current through the path with R_1 is _____ A. the current through the path with

   R_2 is _____ A. The sum of the two individual currents is _____ the current to and from the battery.

   Therefore, in a parallel circuit the _____ of the currents through each path is equal to the total current from the power source.

Rule 4:

4. The total resistance in a parallel circuit is found using the formula: $\frac{1}{R_1} + \frac{1}{R_2} + \frac{1}{R_3} \ldots = \frac{1}{R_1}$

   The total resistance is _____.

Rule 5:

5. At point 3 the circuit is cut. The current _____ continue along the other path.

Physical Science • © Saddleback Educational Publishing • www.sdlback.com

Electric Motors and Generators

Compare an electric motor and an electric generator. Label the magnet, wire loop, commutator, and brush of each device in the diagrams below.

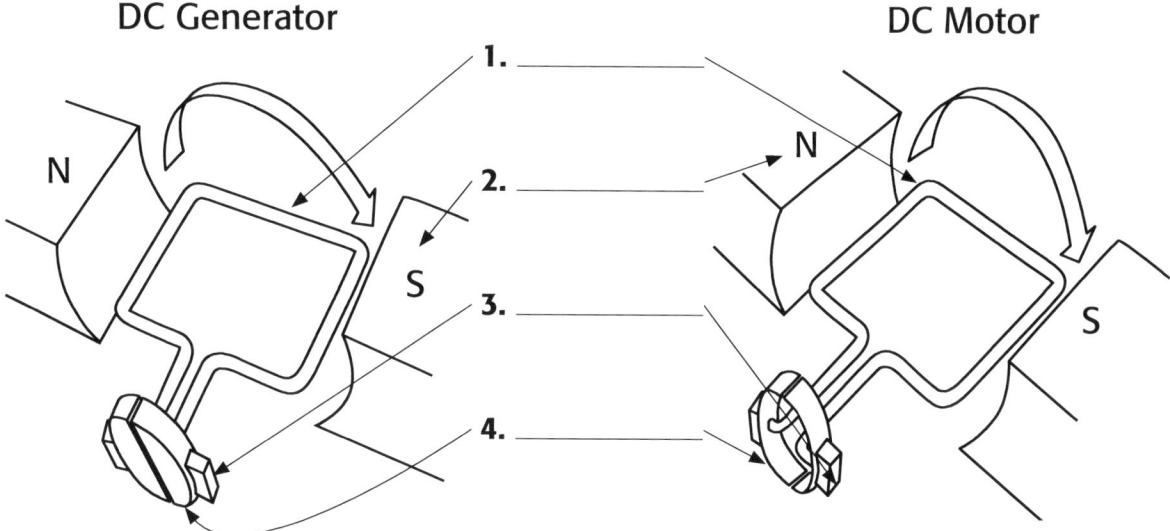

DC Generator   DC Motor

1. _____
2. _____
3. _____
4. _____

Compare an electric motor and an electric generator by completing the table below.

Feature	Electric Motor	Electric Generator
Starts with _____ energy	5.	6.
Converts starting energy to _____ energy	7.	8.
Fixed magnets provide a magnetic field through which a wire coil rotates	9.	10.
Includes a wire loop rotating in a magnetic field	11.	12.
Operates by producing or creating AC current	13.	14.
Operates by producing or creating DC current	15.	16.
Wire loop rotates when current is applied	17.	18.
Supplies current when wire loop rotates	19.	20.
DC version includes a commuter and brushes	21.	22.

Transformers

A transformer is an electrical device that can change the voltage of an AC current to another voltage. Transformers are used to change the high voltage of a current coming into a house to a low voltage needed for many appliances, such as a coffee maker or a toaster.

There are two basic types of transformers, a step-up transformer and a step-down transformer.

Step-up transformer

Current: 10 A   Current: 5 A

Input Volt.: 110 V   Output Volt.: 220 V

Iron Core

Primary coil   Secondary coil
(5 turns)   (10 turns)

Step-down transformer

Current: 10 A   Current: 5 A

Input Volt.: 110 V   Output Volt.: 55 V

Iron Core

Primary coil   Secondary coil
(10 turns)   (5 turns)

Compare a step-up and a step-down transformer by completing the table below.

Feature	Step-up	Step-down
Primary coil?	1.	2.
Secondary coil?	3.	4.
Coil connected to power source	5.	6.
Iron core?	7.	8.
More turns in the primary or secondary?	9.	10.
Higher voltage—output or input?	11.	12.
Lower current—output or input?	13.	14.
Power ($P = VI$)	15.	16.

Calculating Electric Power

Electrical power is the rate that electrical energy is converted to another form of energy in a certain period of time. Explore the nature of electric power. Complete each statement by filling in each blank.

1. The unit of electric power is the _____, which has the symbol _____.

2. Electric power is calculated by multiplying voltage by _____ or $P = VI$.

3. According to the formula for electric power, power (P) and current (I) are

   _____ related. This relationship means that as the current increases

   (with the voltage (V) remaining constant), electric power _____.

4. According to the formula for electric power, voltage (V) and current (I) are

   _____ related. Their relationship means that as the voltage increases

   (with no change in power), the current _____.

Complete the table below regarding the formula for electric power.

Electric Power: $P = VI$		
Variable	**Description**	**Unit**
P	**5.**	**6.**
V	**7.**	**8.**
I	**9.**	**10.**

An oven is connected to 240 V line. The oven uses 40 A of current. What is the power rating of the oven?

Step 1 What do you know?   Voltage (V): 240 V
                                            Current (I): 40 A

Step 2 What are you trying to find?   Power rating (P)

Step 3 What formula can you use? $P = VI$

Step 4 Use the numbers in the formula and solve.   P = (240 V)(40 A)
                                                         P = 9,600 V × A = 9,600 W

11. A coffee maker with a power rating of 600 W uses 5.0 A of current. What is the potential

    difference of the outlet? _____

Energy in the Home

Explore energy use in the home. Use the data in the table below to answer the following questions.

Typical Power Ratings	
Appliance	**Watts**
DVD player	20
Radio	20
Video game player	25
Electric blanket	60
Light bulb	75
Fan	100
Television	110
Computer	120
Refrigerator	700
Microwave	1,000
Clothes dryer	3,000

1. Which activity represents the largest energy use? _____

2. Which activity represents the least energy use? _____

3. A family room has a television, DVD player, and a video game player. How many

   total Watts are used by the devices in the family room? _____

4. How much energy is used when a light bulb runs for 10 hours? (Hint: multiply

   power—in kilowatts—by the time.) _____

5. Electrical energy costs 7.78 cents per kilowatt-hour. How much does it cost to run

   the light bulb for the time given in question 4? (Hint: Multiply the kilowatt-hours

   from question 4 by the cost of electrical energy.)

_____

Answer Key

PAGE 1 *Drawing a Graph*

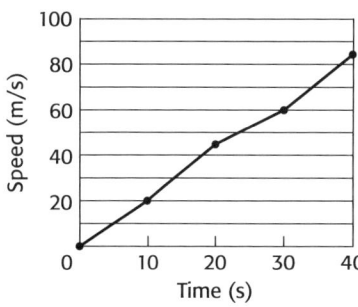

PAGE 2 *Reading a Graph*
1. positive
2. negative
3. no correlation
4. wire length and resistance
5. wire length
6. resistance
7. about 4.3 ohms
8. as the length of the wire increases, the resistance increases
9. positive
10. the resistance will increase to about 8 ohms

PAGE 3 *Organizing Data*
1. Time (min)
2. Water
3. Sand
4. 0 minutes
5. 1 minute
6. 2 minutes
7. 3 minutes
8. 4 minutes
9. 5 minutes

PAGE 4 *Identifying Variables in an Experiment*
1. the type of wood for the ramp, material the marble is made of, the mass of the marble, distance from the bottom of the ramp, height of the ramp
2. the ramp, the marble, the distance from the bottom of the ramp
3. the height of the ramp
4. independent
5. dependent
6. the type of wood for the ramp, material the marble is made of, the mass of the marble, distance from the bottom of the ramp, height of the ramp

PAGE 5 *Designing an Experiment*
1. temperature of the water, time it takes a certain amount of salt to dissolve
2. temperature of the water
3. time it takes the salt to dissolve
4. Material the test tube is made of, location in the lab, Orientation of the test tube, type of thermometer used
5. 3
6. 4
7. 5
8. 1
9. 2

PAGE 6 *Drawing Conclusions*
1. the number of swings decreases from 32 to 23
2. the number of swings decreases from 23 to 17
3. yes
4. the number of swings does not really change
5. yes
6. the number of swings will decrease with increasing length, but will remain the same regardless of the mass

PAGE 7 *Predicting*
1. how the acceleration changes as the mass changes
2. with each increased mass the acceleration decreases
3. Yes, it is negative
4. about 0.5 m/s^2

PAGE 8 *Analyzing Data*
1. voltage and the number of turns on the magnet
2. voltage and number of turns on the magnet
3. number of tacks picked up
4. 3 for the 10-turn magnet and 7 for the 20-turn magnet
5. it increases
6. Yes
7. 3, 7
8. the more turns the more tacks (or the stronger the magnet)

PAGE 9 *Converting SI Units*
1. 1 m
2. 2.5 cg
3. 1 cg
4. 0.00001 km
5. 1,500 m
6. 1.475 g

PAGE 10 *Scientific Method*
1. observation
2. question
3. hypothesis
4. experiment
5. data
6. not supported
7. Revise
8. supports
9. more
10. theory
11. design experiment
12. test hypothesis
13. Pose a question
14. draw conclusion
15. collect data

PAGE 11 *Elements, Compounds, and Mixtures*
1. Pure
2. Uniform, one
3. varied, many
4. Homogeneous
5. can not, atoms
6. can, combined
7. uniform
8. Non- uniform

PAGE 12 *Physical and Chemical Properties*
1. C
2. C
3. P
4. C
5. P
6. P
7. P
8. P
9. C
10. P
11. C
12. C
13. chemical: decomposes to form mercury and oxygen, physical: bright red or red orange, odorless, crystalline solid at room temperature, dissolve in dilute nitric or hydrochloric acid, insoluble in water

PAGE 13 *Physical and Chemical Changes*
1. phase/state
2. dissolving
3. temperature
4. shape
5. smaller
6. gas
7. color
8. solid/precipitate
9. heat

PAGE 14 *Density*
1. 2.6 g/cm^3
2. 2.6 g/cm^3
3. 2.6 g/cm^3
4. 2.6 g/cm^3
5. 2.6 g/cm^3
6. 2.6 g/cm^3
7. 2.6 g/cm^3
8. The mass divided by the volume is approximately the same amount.
9. yes
10. 5.6 g/cm^3
11. 5.6 g/cm^3
12. $48 \text{ g} = M$

PAGE 15 *Solids, Liquids, and Gases*
1. definite
2. varies
3. varies
4. definite
5. definite
6. varies
7. almost none
8. almost none
9. considerable
10. slight
11. moderate
12. readily
13. F, gas
14. T
15. T
16. F, melting
17. F, pressure
18. T
19. T
20. F, crystalline
21. F, gas
22. T

PAGE 16 *Boyle's Law*
1. increased, decreases
2. 75 mL
3. $(75 \text{ mL}) (P_2)$
4. 75
5. 33.67 kPa

PAGE 17 *Charles's Law*
1. increased, decreases
2. 50 mL
3. $\frac{V_1}{T_1} = \frac{V_2}{T_2}$
4. 484K or 213°C

PAGE 18 *The Combined Gas Law*
1. 0.667 L
2. 227 kPa
3. 257K or 14°C

PAGE 19 *Changes of State*
1. Gas
2. F, melting

3. F, will not change
4. T
5. F, apart
6. T
7. F, gas
8. T
9. T

PAGE 20 *Heating Curves*
1. solid
2. increasing
3. continues
4. steady
5. stays the same, melting
6. liquid
7. increasing
8. continues
9. steady
10. stays the same
11. boiling

PAGE 21 *Structure of the Atom*
1. 2nd
2. 3rd
3. 1st
4. 1
5. 1
6. amu
7. $+$
8. $-$
9. nucleus
10. nucleus
11. outside the nucleus
12. p^+
13. n
14. 2
15. e^-
16. 7
17. 2
18. 2
19. 2
20. 8
21. 8
22. 2
23. 2
24. 8
25. 1
26. 2
27. 8
28. 5
29. 2
30. 6

PAGE 22 *Models of Atoms*
1. none
2. atoms
3. electrons, protons
4. electrons
5. positively, electrons
6. nucleus
7. electrons, protons
8. nucleus, electrons
9. electrons, protons

10. nucleus, orbits
11. hydrogen

PAGE 23 *Atomic Mass, Atomic Number, and Isotopes*
1. 30
2. 30
3. Zn
4. 47
5. 60
6. 107
7. Potassium 41
8. 41
9. 41
10. 41
11. 22
12. 12

PAGE 24 *The Periodic Table*
Check that students indicated the proper locations of the metals, nonmetals, metalloids, and noble gases on the periodic table.
1. metals
2. group
3. 22.99
4. non-metals
5. period
6. iodine
7. 26
8. 6
9. transition
10. made in laboratories, radioactive
11. 48

PAGE 25 *Periodic Trends*
1. increased, decreased
2. increases, decreases
3. increases, decreases
4. increases, increases

PAGE 26 *Metals, Nonmetals, and Metalloids*
1. luster
2. Dull
3. dull
4. Good
5. Poor
6. moderate
7. hammered, wire
8. solids
9. ionic, unreactive
10. ionic, 18
11. covalent
12. left
13. right
14. zig-zag
15. Me
16. N
17. Md
18. Md
19. N

20. Me

21. Me

PAGE 27 *Lewis/Electron Dot Structures*

1. 3

2. $\cdot\overset{\cdot}{\underset{}{Al}}\cdot$

3. 8

4. $:\overset{\cdot\cdot}{\underset{\cdot\cdot}{Ar}}:$

5. 7

6. $:\overset{\cdot\cdot}{\underset{\cdot}{Cl}}:$

7. 4

8. $\cdot\overset{}{\underset{\cdot}{Si}}\cdot$

PAGE 28 *Ionic Bonds*

1. 2 lost

2. Ca^{2+}

3. 2 gained

4. O^{2-}

5. CaO

6. 1 lost

7. 3 Na^+

8. 3 gained

9. S^{3-}

10. Na_3S

11. 1 lost

12. H^+

13. 1 gained

14. Cl^-

15. HCl

PAGE 29 *Formulas and Names of Ionic Compounds*

1. LiCl

2. MgF_2

3. $CaCO_3$

4. K_2O

5. $Al(NO_3)_2$

6. beryllium

7. oxygen, oxide

8. beryllium oxide

9. calcium

10. fluorine, fluoride

11. calcium fluoride

PAGE 30 *Covalent Bonds*

1. 7

2. $:\overset{\cdot\cdot}{\underset{\cdot\cdot}{F}}\cdot$ $\overset{xx}{\underset{xx}{F}}x$

3. $:\overset{\cdot\cdot}{\underset{\cdot\cdot}{P}}x\overset{\cdot\cdot}{\underset{}{P}}\cdot$

4. H H $:\overset{\cdot\cdot}{\underset{}{O}}\cdot$

5. $H\cdot\overset{}{\underset{\cdot\cdot}{O}}\cdot H$

6. H H H H

  $\cdot\overset{}{\underset{\cdot}{C}}\cdot$

7. H

  $H\overset{x}{\underset{x}{C}}H$

  H

PAGE 31 *Double and Triple Covalent Bonds*

1. $:\overset{\cdot\cdot}{\underset{}{O}}x x C x\cdot\overset{}{\underset{}{O}}$

2. $H x C x x\cdot C\cdot H$

3. $:\overset{\cdot\cdot}{\underset{}{S}}x x C x\cdot\overset{\cdot\cdot}{\underset{}{S}}$

PAGE 32 *Names of Covalent Compounds*

1. mono

2. 2

3. tri

4. tetra

5. 5

6. hexa

7. 7

8. octa

9. 9

10. deca

11. Di, Pent

12. carbon and fluorine

13. 1 and 4

14. none and tetra

15. carbon tetrafluoride

16. arsenic and oxygen

17. 2 and 3

18. di and tri

19. diarsenic trioxide

20. nitrogen and oxygen

21. 1 and 3

22. none and tri

23. nitrogen trioxide

24. nitrogen and fluorine

25. 1 and 3

26. none and tri

27. nitrogen trifluoride

28. silicon and nitrogen

29. 4 and 4

30. tetra and tetra

31. tetrasilicon tetroxide

32. selenium and oxygen

33. 1 and 2

34. none and di

35. selenium dioxide

PAGE 33 *Mass of a Compound*

1. 1

2. 1

3. 1

4. 23

5. 16

6. 1

7. 23

8. 16

9. 1

10. 40

11. 1

12. 2

13. 24.3

14. 35.5

15. 24.3

16. 70

17. 114.3

18. 6

19. 12

20. 6

21. 12

22. 1

23. 16

24. 72

25. 12

26. 96

27. 180

PAGE 34 *Balancing Chemical Equations*

1. $3H_2 + N_2 - 2NH_3$

2. $2H_2 + O_2 - 2H_2O$

3. $2Al_2O_3 - 4Al + 3O_2$

4. $2SO_2 + O_2 - 2SO_3$

5. $Fe + 2HCl - FeCl_2 + H_2$

PAGE 35 *Classifying Chemical Reactions*

1. one substance

2. One substance

3. element

4. compounds

5. Synthesis

6. double replacement

7. synthesis

8. decomposition

9. single replacement

10. synthesis

11. single replacement

12. double replacement

PAGE 36 *Exothermic and Endothermic Reactions*

1. released

2. Products

3. Reactants

4. absorbed

5. Endo

6. Endo

7. Exo

8. Both

9. Exo

10. Endo

11. Exo

12. Both

13. Exo

PAGE 37 *Chemical Equilibrium*

1. oxygen (O_2)

2. sulfur trioxide (SO_3)

3. right

4. oxygen (O_2)

5. stay the same

6. removes

7. add

8. decreases, fewer

9. increases, greater

10. removes

11. adds

PAGE 38 *Solutions*
 1. T
 2. F, gas-gas
 3. F, decreases
 4. T
 5. T
 6. F, increases
 7. yes
 8. nonpolar
 9. polar/ionic
 10. Nonpolar
 11. alike
 12. increase
 13. will not

PAGE 39 *Solubility Curves*
 1. increase
 2. around 300 g
 3. 30
 4. 100
 5. decreases
 6. $KClO_3$
 7. NH_4Cl

PAGE 40 *Comparing Acids and Bases*
 1. sour
 2. bitter
 3. slippery
 4. hydrogen gas
 5. does not
 6. carbon dioxide
 7. blue
 8. red
 9. yes
 10. yes
 11. hydronium ion – H_3O^+
 12. hydroxide ion – OH^-
 13. A
 14. B
 15. B
 16. A
 17. A
 18. A

PAGE 41 *Strength of Acids and Bases*
 1. WA
 2. SB
 3. WB
 4. SA
 5. SA
 6. A
 7. B
 8. N
 9. A
 10. B
 11. stomach acid, lemon juice, tomato juice, milk, blood, seawater, ammonia

PAGE 42 *Naming Acids and Bases*
 1. 2
 2. 2
 3. 3
 4. 3
 5. hydro
 6. hydro
 7. phosphor
 8. nitr
 9. fluoric acid
 10. chloric acid
 11. ous acid
 12. ic acid
 13. hydrofluoric acid
 14. hydrochloric acid
 15. phosphorous acid
 16. nitric acid

PAGE 43 *Neutralization and Salts*
 1. acid, a base
 2. HCl
 3. $Mg(OH)_2$
 4. $MgCl_2$
 5. ionic
 6. NaOH, HCl
 7. base, acid
 8. H_2CO_3
 9. NaOH
 10. HCl
 11. KOH
 12. HBr
 13. $Mg(OH)_2$

PAGE 44 *Hydrocarbons*
 1. single
 2. C_2H_6–ethane
 3. C_nH_{2n}
 4. –C=C–
 5. triple
 6. H–C≡C–H
 7. 16
 8. 30
 9. 44
 10. 58
 11. 72
 12. 86
 13. 100
 14. 114
 15. 128
 16. 142
 17. methane
 18. decane
 19. increases, increases

PAGE 45 *Substituted Hydrocarbons*
 1. Halogen
 2. Hydroxyl
 3. Ether
 4. Amino
 5. Carbonyl
 6. Carbonyl
 7. Ester
 8. Amido
 9. Carbonyl
 10. Halocarbon
 11. Amine
 12. Ether
 13. Alcohol
 14. Ketone
 15. Aldehyde
 16. Carboxylic acid
 17. Ester

PAGE 46 *Types of Radioactive Decay*
 1. helium
 2. electrons
 3. electromagnetic
 4. ^4_2He
 5. $^0_{-1}\beta$
 6. γ
 7. 2+
 8. 1–
 9. 0
 10. 4, 2
 11. increases
 12. Does not effect the nucleus
 13. paper
 14. metal foil
 15. lead
 16. 226, Radon-222
 17. Uranium, Thorium-234
 18. 131, Xenon-138
 19. Bromine, Krypton-84

PAGE 47 *Nuclear Fission and Fusion*
 1. Fission
 2. Both
 3. Fission
 4. Fusion
 5. Fission
 6. Fission
 7. Fusion
 8. 14
 9. 15
 10. 14

PAGE 48 *Half Life*
 1. half
 2. 5,730
 3. 11,460
 4. about $3\frac{1}{2}$
 5. about 20,000 years old

PAGE 49 *Decay Series*
 1. $^{218}_{84}Po$
 2. $^{214}_{82}Pb$
 3. Beta decay
 4. $^{210}_{82}Pb$
 5. Beta decay
 6. $^{210}_{84}Po$
 7. Alpha decay

PAGE 50 *Graphing Motion*
1. 200 m
2. yes
3. yes
4. 50km/hr

PAGE 51 *Acceleration*
1. increasing
2. positive
3. 0, 10, 10, 10, constant
4. constant
5. 0
6. decreasing, negative
7. 20, 15, 5, 5, constant

PAGE 52 *Balanced and Unbalanced Forces*
1. T
2. F, balanced
3. F, balanced
4. T
5. F, is not needed
6. T
7. 1
8. right
9. 2
10. right
11. 1
12. right
13. 1
14. 2
15. left
16. 1
17. 1
18. down
19. 1
20. down

PAGE 53 *Newton's First Law of Motion*
1. inertia
2. inertia
3. remains at rest
4. continue to move at the same
5. not
6. friction between
7. F, mass
8. F, grams, kilograms
9. T
10. F, may or may not
11. F, inertia
12. W
13. W
14. M
15. W

PAGE 54 *Newton's Second Law of Motion*
1. unbalanced
2. Acceleration
3. acceleration, net force on
4. mass
5. increase

6. decrease
7. m/s^2
8. force
9. increases
10. increases
11. decreases to 52 N
12. decreases
13. decreases
14. increases

PAGE 55 *Calculating Force, Mass, and Acceleration*
1. -12.3 m/s^2

PAGE 56 *Newton's Third Law of Motion*
1. pushes back
2. equal, opposite
3. the same, opposite
4. Earth
5. reaction
6. The road pushes on the car's tire.
7. The gas pushes on the rocket.
8. You pull on a rope attached to a wall.
9. The ball exerts a force on the bat.
10. A hammer exerts a downward force on a nail.

PAGE 57 *Friction*
1. R
2. F
3. All
4. SL
5. St
6. R
7. Sliding
8. overcoming static friction

PAGE 58 *Gravity*
1. F, weakest
2. T
3. T
4. F, stronger
5. T
6. F, an attractive
7. F, downward towards
8. T
9. T
10. 180.5
11. 441.5
12. 490
13. 187.5
14. 1300
15. 61.2
16. 525
17. 665
18. 30.5

PAGE 59 *Momentum*
1. F, velocity
2. T
3. T

4. F, same
5. F, harder
6. T
7. F, lower
8. 4 kg object moving at 1.2 m/s

PAGE 60 *Conservation of Momentum*
1. stick
2. at rest
3. stops, moves
4. in motion
5. rebound, opposite to
6. the same
7. slower, faster
8. stick
9. moving, at rest
10. lower
11. $1\frac{1}{3}$ m/s

PAGE 61 *Calculating Work*
1. newtons
2. does not
3. joule
4. does
5. does not
6. 168.5 J

PAGE 62 *Mechanical Advantage*
1. T
2. F, input distance
3. F, ideal
4. T
5. F, meters or any unit of length
6. 4

PAGE 63 *Simple Machines*
1. b
2. d
3. f
4. c
5. a
6. e
7. 14.2
8. 7.69
9. 5.26
10. 3.70
11. the 5.0/0.35 m ramp
12. the 5.0/0.35 m ramp
13. the 5.0/1.35 m ramp
14. The mechanical advantage decreases

PAGE 64 *Types of Levers*
1. opposite
2. between
3. the opposite
4. between
5. input force
6. the same
7. between
8. output force
9. the same
10. ↓

11. ≠
12. input force
13. input force
14. ≠
15. fulcrum

PAGE 65 *Fixed and Movable*
Pulleys

1. M
2. A
3. S
4. S
5. F
6. F
7. M
8. F
9. 1
10. 1
11. 2
12. 2
13. 3
14. 2
15. 2
16. pulley system
17. 15 N

PAGE 66 *Pascal's Principle*

1. equally
2. increases, 10
3. hydraulic
4. multiplies
5. weight
6. larger
7. smaller
8. 2,700

PAGE 67 *Bernoulli's Principle*

1. decreases
2. inversely
3. the same as
4. the same as
5. greater than
6. less than
7. Section A and Section C,
   Section B
8. less than
9. greater than
10. Section B, Section C, Section A
11. higher, slower

PAGE 68 *Kinetic and*
Potential Energy

1. B
2. K
3. P
4. P
5. B
6. K
7. P
8. B
9. 0.74
10. 0.74
11. 0.74

12. 0.74
13. 0.74
14. resting
15. is not
16. decreases
17. increases, increases
18. stays the same, conservation

PAGE 69 *Calculating*
Kinetic Energy

1. in motion
2. mass, velocity
3. double
4. quadruple
5. mass, kg
6. velocity, m/s
7. joules
8. 480000 J

PAGE 70 *Calculating Gravitational*
Potential Energy

1. F, position
2. T
3. T
4. F, mass
5. F, kg
6. F, meters
7. T
8. 825 J

PAGE 71 *Forms of Energy*

1. d
2. e
3. b
4. a
5. f
6. c
7. El
8. M
9. C
10. Em
11. N
12. M
13. thermal
14. chemical
15. nuclear
16. chemical

PAGE 72 *Calculating Power*

1. rate
2. more, increase
3. less
4. joules
5. seconds
6. watts
7. doubling, half
8. 800 J

PAGE 73 *Temperature and*
Temperature Scales

1. 100
2. 373
3. 98.6

4. 310
5. 20
6. 293
7. 32
8. 0
9. Kelvin
10. Celsius
11. twice
12. absolute zero
13. –3.89°C
14. 59°F
15. 22.8°C
16. 214°F

PAGE 74 *Heat Transfer*

1. Cv
2. Rd
3. Rd
4. Cd
5. Cv
6. Rd
7. Cd
8. Cv
9. conductors
10. good
11. poor
12. insulators
13. gases
14. radiant
15. collision
16. liquids

PAGE 75 *Specific Heat*

1. one, one
2. water
3. silver
4. low
5. 881 J

PAGE 76 *Laws of*
Thermodynamics

1. 2nd
2. 3rd
3. 1st
4. 2nd
5. 2nd
6. 1st
7. 15 J

PAGE 77 *Heat Engines*

1. heat
2. Work
3. heat
4. heat
5. Work
6. heat
7. high, lower
8. exhaust
9. 153.3 J, 51.2 J, 204.5 J
10. cold, hot
11. 1,000 J, 200 J, 1,200 J

PAGE 78 *Properties of Waves*
1. wavelength
2. crest
3. Rest position
4. wavelength
5. trough
6. amplitude
7. b
8. e
9. c
10. f
11. d
12. g
13. a
14. 2 hertz
15. decreases
16. frequency
17. greater

PAGE 79 *Types of Waves*
1. T
2. All
3. T
4. L
5. S
6. L
7. All
8. wavelength
9. crest
10. direction of wave
11. Direction of displacement
12. trough
13. wavelength
14. Compression
15. Direction of displacement
16. Rarefraction
17. direction of wave

PAGE 80 *Calculating Wave Speed*
1. F meters or centimeters
2. F, hertz
3. T
4. F, increases
5. T
6. T
7. 0.375 m/s

PAGE 81 *Wave Interference*
1. add together
2. destructive
3. Constructive
4. increased, constructive
5. crest, crest
6. trough, trough
7. crest, crest
8. same, added
9. 3, –3, 3

PAGE 82 *Wave Reflection and Refraction*
1. Incident
2. Reflected

3. incidence
4. reflection
5. incident
6. reflected
7. incidence
8. reflection
9. equals
10. Incident
11. Incident
12. Reflected
13. Reflected
14. away
15. towards
16. slower
17. faster

PAGE 83 *Properties of Sound*
1. F, longitudinal
2. T
3. T
4. F, intensity
5. F, amplitude
6. T
7. F, decibels
8. T
9. aluminum, air at 0°C
10. faster
11. fastest, gases
12. closer

PAGE 84 *The Doppler Effect*
1. F, equal
2. T
3. F, point D, point C
4. F, shorter
5. T
6. F, higher
7. T

PAGE 85 *Electromagnetic Spectrum*
1. food irradiation, material examination
2. heat lamps
3. microwave ovens
4. radio and television
5. sterilized medical materials
6. visible light application
7. medical examination
8. radio waves, gamma rays
9. radio waves, gamma rays
10. lower, inversely
11. ultraviolet light

PAGE 86 *Concave Mirrors*
1. inwardly
2. reflects
3. focal, real
4. upside down
5. straight
6. focal
7. focal
8. center of the curvature

PAGE 87 *Convex Mirrors*
1. outwardly
2. reflects
3. focal
4. behind
5. real, upright
6. straight
7. focal
8. focal
9. parallel

PAGE 88 *Concave Lenses*
1. thin, thick
2. diverges
3. outward
4. same
5. virtual
6. upright
7. straight
8. back
9. straight, center
10. straight

PAGE 89 *Convex Lenses*
1. thick, thin
2. diverges
3. inward
4. focal
5. real
6. upside down
7. straight
8. focal
9. center
10. center
11. focal
12. straight

PAGE 90 *Color*
1. F, reflected
2. F, white
3. F, black
4. T
5. T
6. T
7. F, white
8. yellow
9. magenta
10. white
11. blue

PAGE 91 *Magnets and Magnetism*
1.

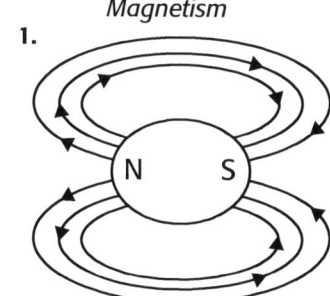

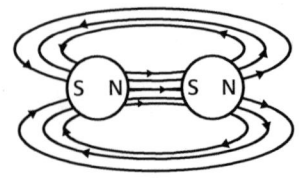

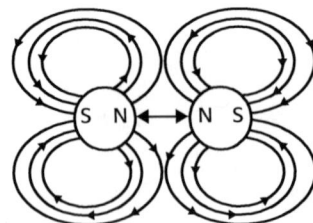

2. repel
3. attract
4. attract
5. repel
6. poles
7. two
8. attract
9. repel
10. two
11. pole

PAGE 92 *Electric Charges*

1.

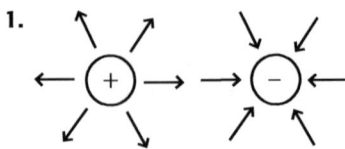

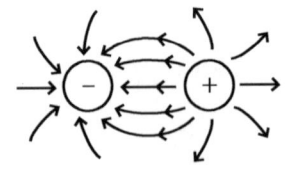

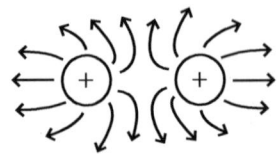

2. Attract
3. Repel
4. Repel
5. Attract
6. T
7. F, repel
8. F, electrons
9. F, positively
10. T
11. T

PAGE 93 *Ohm's Law*
1. ampere
2. voltage
3. current
4. increase
5. decrease
6. voltage
7. Volts (V)
8. current
9. Ampere (A)
10. resistance
11. Ohms (Ω)
12. 22.5 V

PAGE 94 *Electric Circuits—Introduction*
1. f
2. d
3. a
4. c
5. g
6. e
7. b
8. Resistor
9. Power Source
10. Bulb
11. Closed switch
12.

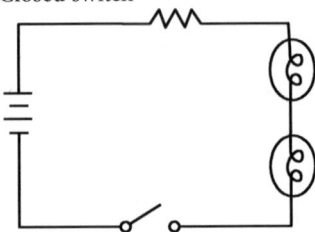

PAGE 95 *Series Circuits*
1. connected
2. negative, positive
3. same
4. 5 Ω, 5 Ω, 10 Ω, sum
5. 20 V, 20 V sum
6. no

PAGE 96 *Parallel Circuits*
1. current, more than
2. the same
3. 1, 1, equal to, sum
4. $\frac{1}{10} + \frac{1}{10} = \frac{2}{10} = \frac{1}{5} = 0.20\ \Omega$
5. will

PAGE 97 *Electric Motors and Generators*
1. Wire Loop
2. Magnet
3. Brush
4. Commutator

5. electrical
6. mechanical
7. mechanical
8. electrical
9. yes
10. yes
11. yes
12. yes
13. yes
14. yes
15. yes
16. yes
17. yes
18. no
19. no
20. yes
21. yes
22. yes

PAGE 98 *Transformers*
1. yes
2. yes
3. yes
4. yes
5. primary
6. primary
7. yes
8. yes
9. secondary
10. primary
11. output
12. input
13. output
14. input
15. $P = 110\ V \times 10\ A = 1,100\ W$
16. $P = 55\ V \times 20\ A = 1,100\ W$

PAGE 99 *Calculating Electric Power*
1. watt, W
2. current
3. directly, increase
4. inversely, decreases
5. power
6. watt (W)
7. voltage
8. volts (V)
9. current
10. amperes (A)
11. 120 V

PAGE 100 *Energy in the Home*
1. clothes dryer
2. DVD player and radio
3. 155 W
4. 0.075 kW × 10 h = 0.75 kW • h
5. 0.75 kW • h × $0.778 = $0.58